Manifest with t
Astro-Moon Di

from the I Choose Love Series.
The Pathway of the Spiritual Warrior.

Manifest with the Moon
Astro-Moon Diary 2023

This Diary Belongs to

....

Manifest with the Moon Astro-Moon Diary 2023
From the I Choose Love Series
The Pathway of the Spiritual Warrior

Manifest with the Moon Astro-Moon Diary & Journal
The Art of Manifestation Astro-Moon Diary & Journal
First Published 2019 A-Z of Emotional Health Ltd.

Published by the A-Z of Emotional Health Ltd.

Isbn - 978-1-8382863-4-7

The intent of the author is only to offer information of a general nature to assist in an individual's search for emotional and spiritual wellness. In the event that you use any of the information in this book for yourself, the author and publisher assume no responsibility for your actions.

Contents

Manifest with the Moon

Astro-Moon Diary 2023

For extra Moon information & webinars follow Jenny on social media

- https://www.youtube.com/c/MoonMagicWeeklyTarot
- https://www.facebook.com/MoonMagicJennyFlorence
- https://www.instagram.com/moonmagicjennyflorence/

The Art of Manifestation

Having worked as an Accredited UK registered Counsellor for over 28 years, I have had the privilege to walk alongside literally hundreds of people, who despite facing major stuff in their personal lives, through deep diving into their own psychology and emotions, were able to overcome their difficulties and move their lives forward, and so I have a passion to explore any tools that can help us to transform and manifest, and this is what started my own magical journey of learning to manifest with the Moon.

Manifestation isn't just about imagining and dreaming about the life you want; you will also need to take actions so that your dreams can find form, and whilst some things can arrive very quickly, other things take time, spiraling through many phases of the manifestation process.

It seems to me that manifestation follows a natural cyclical pattern and when I started to seriously follow the phases of the Moon, I realized that the influence of the incoming Lunar flow of energy perfectly mirrored the different stages of manifestation.

As I explored the Moon phases further I found that the influence of the zodiac sign that the Moon was passing through also had a noticeable effect on the way that I was thinking and feeling.

Learning how the Lunar energy was effecting me personally changed my take on manifestation completely and opened up a whole new way of living... more effectively... more fruitfully... more productively... more peacefully... and more spiritually... in fact, all aspects of my life, both personally and professionally, have changed for the better!

So, let's take a look at the phases of manifestation, and then the phases of the Moon, the parallel is amazing!

The Phases of Manifestation

1. You decide you want something, and you give yourself permission to believe in this possibility and to dream.
2. Now you will need to take some sort of steps towards this, whether big or small... and commit to moving forwards and doing what it takes.
3. Review and ongoing evaluation will be needed, manifestation happens one step at a time!
4. Excitement and energy builds... you commit, you invest, and you persevere.
5. As progress unfolds, whether in your external actions or deep within our own psyche, the universe will show you what is needed to keep your energy flowing. So, you'll need to observe and listen... what is working and what isn't? And then actively use this information to validate your purpose and direction... and if needed, cleanse and release so you can commit fully to the journey ahead.
6. Holding a clarity of mind, you are now wiser and stronger, you continue with steady progress.
7. In steady momentum, trusting that the universe knows your fullest potential and holds a higher vision that is greater than you could possibly imagine, remember to pause, and evaluate along the way... there is always opportunity to make adjustments and tweak the details.
8. As your pathway emerges and your dreams begin to take form, remember to slow down, and enjoy the journey. Life is for living and being too fixed on the future can actually slow your manifestations down! Be balanced... slow and steady wins the race... and periods of stillness will often open avenues of new potential.

And a new cycle begins... you listen to your desires and give yourself permission to believe and to dream. Some of your manifestations will be ongoing, with a new phase building on the foundation of the last... whilst others will be completely new, fresh ideas born of experiences that forge new desires.

The Phases of the Moon

1. The New Moon is traditionally associated with the setting of wishes and intentions and the energy naturally invites you to dream of possibilities.
2. In the phase of the Crescent Moon the seeds that emerged at the New Moon call to be heard. In manifestation, we are both doers and deciders… it's time to respond and be proactive in taking steps, however small or large.
3. The First Quarter Moon is a time of evaluation, so look carefully at the scope of your ideas and use this energy to focus on the actions that are most important at this moment in time… review and formulate your goals for the rest of the month.
4. In the Gibbous Moon phase energy is building, passions are high, and dreams call to be made real. Enjoy the excitement of anticipation but remain present and grounded. Commit, invest, and persevere.
5. The brightness and power of the highly charged Full Moon energy brings a space of authenticity where all is revealed and illuminated, so notice and listen, particularly to any situations that seem to demand your attention. The energy of this phase of the Moon brings a wonderful opportunity to notice, to listen, to reflect, and then to release and let go, clearing the way to move forwards.
6. The Disseminating Moon phase invites authentic empowerment. Be steady in your actions and in your doings, stand in your power and be your true self with joy, gratitude, and humility, and affirm your dedication to your pathway.
7. The energy of the Last Quarter Moon invites you to walk your talk, so stand back and review, and make sure your plans, actions, and decisions are congruent with all that you wish to see in the world, and if need be, tweak and adjust.
8. The Balsamic Moon asks you to trust. Hold your vision, and yet simultaneously let go of any attachment to specific outcomes. This is a time of preparation and nurture. Validate, acknowledge, and cherish all your achievements and as this Lunar cycle comes to its completion prepare the ground for your own deliverance and the beginning of a new cycle of opportunity.

And a new cycle begins… you listen to your desires and give yourself permission to believe and to dream. Some of your manifestations will be ongoing, with a new phase building on the foundation of the last… whilst others will be completely new, fresh ideas born of experiences that forge new desires.

How to Use this Diary

Knowing about the ebb and flow and flavor of the incoming Lunar lens ahead of time, is a major tool of empowerment. When I started to follow the Moon phases on a daily basis I realized very quickly that the incoming Lunar energy was touching and influencing my emotions and my thoughts, and even my physical wellbeing as well, and especially my energy levels… all of which then affected my overall attitude, mood, and state of mind. I could see tangible variations in how relaxed I was feeling… or how stressed I was… whether I felt confident, resilient, and durable, or ultra-sensitive and far more vulnerable… whether I felt motivated or stuck… focused or all over the place… all of this and more, even though my actual circumstances hadn't necessarily changed.

So, I started to make notes about the way that the incoming Lunar energy was affecting me personally and these notes became a reference point for me.

The Moon always follows a consistent pattern, sometimes increasing and accelerating, and sometimes diminishing and easing, with peaks of greater intensity along the way. This energy is then in turn flavored by the personality and characteristics of the Zodiac sign that the Moon is passing through, creating a kind of the 'Lunar Lens' of the day. This is also influenced further as the Moon passes by and connects with the other major planetary alignments that are happening. And the phases of the Moon also happen to align perfectly with the stages of manifestation.

This diary is a tool.

As the saying goes 'Knowledge is Power' and in my personal experience, the more awareness you have of the incoming flow of Lunar energy, the more empowered you are. It's like having a really good personal GPS that lets you know ahead of time about any speed limits… whether the flow of traffic is fast and unrestricted… or busy but steady… or if there are roadworks and diversions ahead… you'll need to slow down… or even take a different route!

This diary is designed to give you exactly the information you need to build a personal record of how the Moon is affecting you individually so that you can align your daily living and ongoing manifestations with the incoming energy of the Moon. The week to view pages tell you the phase and zodiac sign of the Moon each day with space for you to record your own experiences.

At the beginning of each month, you'll find a run-down of the Lunar influence for each phase of the Moon so you're ultra-prepped for what is coming… and there's even some additional guidance from Oracle Cards and Runes to help you navigate with awareness. And at the back you'll find a ton of extra information, including a description of the way that the lunar energy is affected and channeled as the Moon travels through each sign of the zodiac signs, what the Void of Course Moon means (VOC – you'll see this in the diary pages), the influence of Solar and Lunar eclipses, and the planets in retrograde, with listings of the dates that these events occur.

And if you're really serious about manifesting with the Moon you may also wish to use the Manifest with the Moon Astro-Moon Journal which takes you into a whole other layer of Moon magic! In this Moon journal, drawing on the wisdom of Celtic Tree Lore and Tribal Traditions, I'll tell you about the deeper psychological Soul growth layer of monthly Moon magic that has been understand for centuries by our ancestors, and for me was absolutely life changing!

Desires, Goals, and Intentions for January 2023

(1) Respond rather react - in all ways especially at MC/DMC meetings.

(2) Good nutrition & health.

(3) Drink more water.

[set these on 8/1/23]

Every life experience, the good, the bad and everything in between, is actually an entry point into newer and higher levels of consciousness.

Welcome to January 2023

January 2023. Completions and New Beginnings.

The year of 2023 begins with the Moon in her Waxing Gibbous phase, building in energy and momentum, which peaks at the Full Moon in Cancer on January 6th / 7th inviting you to listen and observe. The Super New Moon in Aquarius, also Lunar Imbolc in the northern hemisphere, on January 21st / 22nd invites transformation and re-birth... and with turbo charged momentum... so, from a Lunar perspective, you may well notice a very tangible shift between the old and the new with areas of your world coming to the fore that support the completions of 2022 whilst simultaneously creating new directions and a new focus for your dreams, goals, and ambitions of 2023.

In terms of manifestation, with the month beginning with Mercury, Mars, and Uranus still in retrograde, the overall astro-dynamics of January invite you to steady up and set aside pockets of real time to review where you are right now, tie up any loose ends, deal with any unfinished business, and with clean energy and a refreshed viewpoint, lean into a space of new potentials.

The flow of energy through the month is distinct...

- Consolidation and evaluation...
- Get still and get clear...
- Hold a realistic vision...
- Respond rather than re-act...
- Transformation is key...
- Karmic directions...
- Go with the flow...
- Let the Universe guide you...

Our Cards this month of Believe in Yourself and Nurture alongside Kano the Rune of Openings and Ehwaz, the Rune of Movement, invite you to hold steady, release any inner blocks to progress, nurture rather than push, and work with the natural flow and momentum, as we shift into a space of new unfolding.

Cards and Runes January 2023

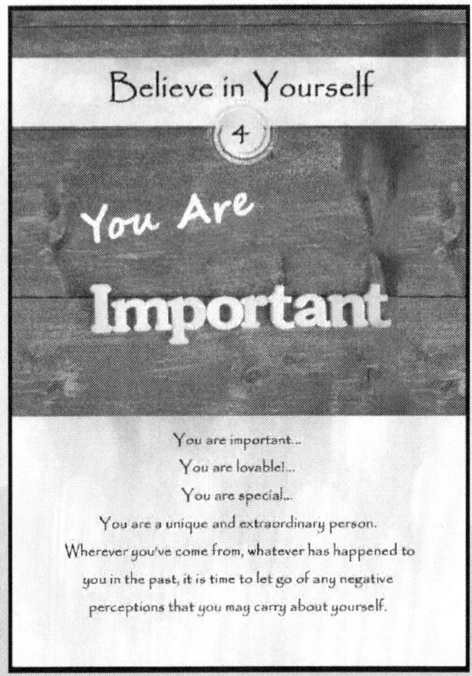

Kano the Rune of Openings indicates a time of potential for renewed clarity bringing clear intentions and significant personal empowerment. Combined with the card of Believe in Yourself you are invited to let go of any internal beliefs that have previously held you back and see yourself as the source of change in your life.

Additional messages and guidance.
Low self-esteem is far more common than you might believe. A great many people struggle to believe in themselves, holding deep seated negative or limiting beliefs about themselves. These perspectives stem from earlier experiences, usually in childhood.

If you have faced difficulties in your formative years then this is completely understandable, however it is essential in adult life that we challenge these inner beliefs and empower ourselves to move beyond these limitations. Let go of any negative perceptions that you may carry about yourself and if necessary, seek counselling or coaching to support you in this process.

Cards and Runes January 2023

Ehwaz the Rune of Movement indicates the bettering of any situation and is an indication of a significant period of transition that validates your progress and suggests movement, growth, and the gathering of momentum which combined with the Card of Nurture invites you to invest in your future plans and ambitions with confidence and determination.

Additional messages and guidance.

Drawing this card is an indication that you have sown seeds and may be experiencing a degree of frustration and impatience, potentially leading to self-doubt as to whether or not your relationship/idea/project is going to develop and move forwards as you hope.

This card brings reassurance that you have made a wise choice and a wise investment and that your hard work is going to pay off. Whatever you have begun, you are called to be patient and to nurture your situation with love. Your hopes and your dreams are developing more quickly than you realize.

Moon Phases January 2023

The Waxing Gibbous Moon – from December 31st - January 5th passing through Aries, Taurus, Gemini, and into Cancer.

Despite beginning the year with both Mercury and Mars in retrograde positions, which can herald interruptions and disruption, the overall energy during this Moon phase is remarkably flowing. Steady and yet dynamic! There are a couple of spikes of greater intensity around the 2nd and the 5th, so in your manifestation progress the Lunar flow favors perseverance with consistent steady action whilst simultaneously remaining flexible. Be responsive if any unexpected situations and circumstances arise, even if they interrupt your flow and create disruption, they are here to initiate evaluation and review, highlighting any areas where adjustments are needed.

The Full Moon - January 6th / 7th - 16° 21’ Cancer.

A Full Moon illuminates to help you see the right way forward and this can involve letting go and/or making adjustments. Today’s Full Moon in Cancer sits directly opposite Mercury in retrograde, naturally inviting you to slow down and observe. A Cancer Moon puts you in touch with emotions, highlighting areas of life related to nurture, care, (including self-care) family, and home, and this Moon is emotionally intense. So, use this powerful time to consciously slow down, listen, observe, and review. Take an inventory of your personal life, right here and right now. Honor your feelings, commit to a pathway of healthy self-care and the letting go of anything that inhibits this process, and pledge to a year of manifestations that spring from the heart rather than the head.

Full Moon Global Timings:

Los Angeles, USA	Fri, 6 Jan 2023 at 15:07 PST
New York, USA	Fri, 6 Jan 2023 at 18:07 EST
Reykjavik, Iceland	Fri, 6 Jan 2023 at 23:07 GMT
London, United Kingdom	Fri, 6 Jan 2023 at 23:07 GMT
Paris, France	Sat, 7 Jan 2023 at 00:07 CET
Cape Town, South Africa	Sat, 7 Jan 2023 at 01:07 SAST
Delhi, India	Sat, 7 Jan 2023 at 04:37 IST
Perth, Australia	Sat, 7 Jan 2023 at 07:07 AWST
Tokyo, Japan	Sat, 7 Jan 2023 at 08:07 JST
Sydney, Australia	Sat, 7 Jan 2023 at 10:07 AEDT
Auckland, New Zealand	Sat, 7 Jan 2023 at 12:07 NZDT
Greenwich Mean Time, GMT	Fri, 6 Jan 2023 at 23:07 GMT

The Disseminating or Waning Gibbous Moon – from January 8th – 13th passing through Leo, Virgo, and into Libra.

For me, in terms of successful manifesting, the overall flow of Lunar energy during this period requires clarity of intent. There is a spike of energy on the 10th which fosters very solid growth but could also require you to face facts and get real! If this is the case, then use this information to inform you, and invest your time and energy wisely. Mercury is still in retrograde, so hold your longer-term vision, and be steady on your course.

This is a good time to lay foundations and to lay them well with attention to detail. A solid foundation creates a resilient and durable future. Mars stands still on 12th, but we also see a spike of Lunar energy that could be quite emotionally intense, so if you feel a bit wobbly, just ride the waves and flow into the energy of the 13th which suggests the potential for a significant shift forwards, fostering rebalance, realignment, and calmer waters.

The Last Quarter Moon – January 14th / 15th – Libra.

The Last Quarter Moon invites you to step up, walk your talk, and be the change that you wish to see in the world. The overall Lunar dynamics at this Last Quarter Moon in Libra suggest an intensity, moving from a space of sudden evaluation to a place where action is called for, almost with a sense of urgency. Events that surface may well demand a response, particularly in situations that feel unjust or unfair. In terms of spiritual Soul growth, these events are here to strengthen and build a resilient and durable inner foundation based on personal congruence and authenticity. So, in short… whatever is happening in your world, step up and be yourself, with openness, honesty, and integrity and the Universe will support you.

The Balsamic Moon or Waning Crescent Moon – from January 16th – 20th passing through Scorpio, Sagittarius, and into Capricorn.

This Moon phase begins with a distinctly karmic flavor! During this period, you may well be shown opportunities to shift your perspectives, so you can view all sides of the story and keep the bigger picture in mind, creating new ways of seeing, doing and being. With the Sun entering Aquarius on the 20th, you may well be shown everything you need to know to create sound and dynamic New Moon wishes and intentions for the first New Moon of 2023 on January 21st. This coming New Moon is a Moon of ambition, rebirth and emergence so fasten your seatbelts and use this Balsamic Waning Moon phase to get clear. This is an important time for observation, reflection, and preparation.

The Super New Moon - January 21st / 22nd - 1° 32' Aquarius.

The dynamics of this first New Moon of 2023 are extraordinarily powerful in terms of transformation and momentum! It is also the Moon of the Lunar Imbolc in the northern hemisphere. The Sun and the Moon unite and join forces with the transformational energy of Pluto suggesting profound opportunities for re-birth. The collaboration of these three then sit directly opposite Lilith who fights for the underdog and calls us to address any issues of injustice and inequality! This dynamic is then infused with the fiery go-getting energy of Mars and the expansive energy of Jupiter. So, what does this all actually mean...

If things are going well in your world and you have been working to create dynamic change then the energy today supports you wholeheartedly! Expect swift and powerful openings. However, things that are not running quite so smoothly could come to a head with circumstances that ask for change and a swift response. This is a good time to touch base with the messages from our Cards and Runes this month... nurture rather than push, and work with the natural flow and momentum!

New Moon Global Timings:

Los Angeles, USA	Sat, 21 Jan 2023 at 12:53 PST
New York, USA	Sat, 21 Jan 2023 at 15:53 EST
Reykjavik, Iceland	Sat, 21 Jan 2023 at 20:53 GMT
London, United Kingdom	Sat, 21 Jan 2023 at 20:53 GMT
Paris, France	Sat, 21 Jan 2023 at 21:53 CET
Cape Town, South Africa	Sat, 21 Jan 2023 at 22:53 SAST
Delhi, India	Sun, 22 Jan 2023 at 02:23 IST
Perth, Australia	Sun, 22 Jan 2023 at 04:53 AWST
Tokyo, Japan	Sun, 22 Jan 2023 at 05:53 JST
Sydney, Australia	Sun, 22 Jan 2023 at 07:53 AEDT
Auckland, New Zealand	Sun, 22 Jan 2023 at 09:53 NZDT
Greenwich Mean Time, GMT	Sat, 21 Jan 2023 at 20:53 GMT

The Waxing Crescent Moon – from January 23rd – 27th passing through Aquarius, Pisces, and into Aries.

Following such an intense and dynamic New Moon, and with the sometimes-erratic energy of Uranus now standing still after a long period of retrograde energy, initially the Lunar influence of this phase is remarkably steady, suggesting consistent emergence and progression, so invest in your manifestations at a reliable pace. As the Moon moves through Pisces the Lunar influence is productively dreamy so if you have trouble holding your focus, then ease back until clarity arrives. When the Moon passes into Aries the flow and pace looks to speed up and accelerate.

The First Quarter Moon – January 28th - Taurus.

Today the Moon aligns with the karmic influence of the Nodes. This collaboration is said to bring guidance that supports you in finding your direction, purpose, and calling. Given that the Lunar energy at the Quarter Moon positions offers a natural point of review and evaluation, whatever is happening in your world, pay particular attention to any signs and synchronicities and take them seriously.

The Waxing Gibbous Moon – from January 29th into February passing through Taurus into Gemini.

We finish January with the Moon moving into her Waxing Gibbous phase and building in strength and momentum. For the best part of this Moon phase the energy gates are open... so get into the flow and don't hold back! If you find a brief hiccup or hurdle on the 30th just lean into the energy and trust there is a purpose to this, it will soon pass as we move into February.

26 Monday
Aquarius / VOC

Boxing Day
Waxing Crescent Moon Phase

27 Tuesday
VOC / Pisces

Bank Holiday - UK Christmas Day Substitute

28 Wednesday I went to Bournemouth
Pisces

29 Thursday
Pisces / VOC / Aries

Mercury Retrograde Begins
Waxing Crescent Moon Phase Ends

30 Friday Andrea & I went to Glastonbury.
Aries I thought we were going for the
day but we stayed over night.
I felt coerced by her sister to
this - I wasn't consulted as to
First Quarter Moon Aries whether I wanted to do this

Journaling and Notes

31 Saturday
Aries / VOC / Taurus

New Year's Eve
Waxing Gibbous Moon Phase Begins

1 Sunday
Taurus

New Year's Day

2 Monday I came back to London

Taurus / VOC

Bank Holiday - UK New Year's Day Substitute

---

3 Tuesday

VOC / Gemini

---

4 Wednesday

Gemini

---

5 Thursday

Gemini / VOC / Cancer

I felt quite emotional this evening.

Waxing Gibbous Moon Phase Ends

---

6 Friday Spent 9 - 6pm almost

Cancer solidly writing the 1st

RMA w/end.

Full Moon 16°21' Cancer

Journaling and Notes

Saturday - didn't feel well all night - stomach not happy, I think too much fat - butter/oil in the evening meal & too much alcohol.
I had 3 glasses wine & 1 gin.

↑

7 Saturday
Cancer / VOC

Lesley came - she is very heavy energy.
I cooked roast chicken tonight - Butternut squash, Green veg, but had too much alcohol - went to bed at 10.30pm.

Full Moon 16°21' Cancer

8 Sunday
VOC / Leo

Tummy not right - a lot of poo & uncomfortable.
Can feel a small lump on left side of upper stomach under the breast - slightly concerned I might have an ulcer.

Waning Gibbous Moon Phase Begins

9 Monday
Leo

Started supervisee, client work today after the holiday. I feel good.

10 Tuesday
Leo / VOC / Virgo

Woke up at 10am – V. unusual – even on days off I am usually up at 8.30pm – It was good weather yesterday but a lot of rain today. Also started work again yesterday – perhaps that is why I am tired?

11 Wednesday
Virgo

This afternoon eve, noticed my right foot painful on the right side – + clicking – a bit painful to walk – some kind of injury.

↓

12 Thursday
Virgo / VOC

Woke up at 3.15am – foot hurts & has swelling – need a bandage – can't find one. V. stormy outside – big wind & rain

Mars Retrograde Ends

13 Friday
VOC / Libra

1st RMA 2023 Day

Went well.

Waning Gibbous Moon Phase Ends

Journaling and Notes

14 Saturday
Libra

1st RMA Research weekend.

I think it went well

Last Quarter Moon Libra

15 Sunday
Libra / VOC / Scorpio

Today someone had a melt down re ethics!

Last Quarter Moon Libra

16 Monday
Scorpio

Martin Luther King Jr. Day - USA
Waning Crescent Moon Phase Begins

17 Tuesday
Scorpio / VOC / Sagittarius

1st dreams group
with 3 new people
– went well.

18 Wednesday
Sagittarius

Mercury Retrograde Ends

19 Thursday
Sagittarius / VOC / Capricorn

20 Friday
Capricorn

7–8.30pm EDI RMA
lecture – went
well.

Sun Enters Aquarius
Waning Crescent Moon Phase Ends

Journaling and Notes

on Saturday morning had
2 Mushroom Coffees -
Felt V. alert but also
relaxed not stressed -
Usually when I am around
Lesley I can feel stressed.

21 Saturday

Capricorn / VOC / Aquarius

Went to Lesley's lock up - a lot less in there than she thought. Had a Macdonalds Around 5pm exhausted. Had a couple hours rest & OK.

Lunar Imbolc – Northern Hemisphere
Super New Moon 1°32' Aquarius

22 Sunday

Aquarius

Lunar Imbolc – Northern Hemisphere
Super New Moon 1°32' Aquarius
Uranus Retrograde Ends

23 **Monday**
Aquarius / VOC / Pisces

Waxing Crescent Moon Phase Begins

24 **Tuesday**
Pisces

So I went to bed at 11am last night,
Woke up & couldn't sleep at 3.30-4am.
1/2 hr Cup of tea. knew I was
tired - but didn't get bk to sleep
for about 1 hour. Had to get up
at 7am to get to CCPE for dreams
group - had 3 coffees - too much.

25 **Wednesday**
Pisces / VOC Aries

26 **Thursday**
Aries

Australia Day

27 **Friday**
Aries / VOC / Taurus

Waxing Crescent Moon Phase Ends

Journaling and Notes

Got home at 4pm - big headache - tired. Just realised that the moon is in Pisces. At MC said goodbye to Angela - v. sad. Then upset as Paul Margne hadn't invited me to his retirement on Sat. He does not like me. Over emotional on bus - my parents don't like me, no-one likes me, something wrong with me etc. At least I didn't 'lose' it at DMC/MC...

V. emotional &

V. tired -

bought bread & pizza...

28 **Saturday**

Taurus

First Quarter Moon Taurus

29 **Sunday**

Taurus

Waxing Gibbous Moon Phase Begins

Desires, Goals, and Intentions for February 2023

Welcome to February 2023

February 2023. Moving Things Forward.

From a Lunar perspective, February feels like a month that offers the potential for consistent progress with pockets of Lunar flow that bring moments of reflection and greater clarity, intermixed with surges of renewal to further progress. To make the very best of the these influences I would suggest reading through the Moon Phases ahead of time and plan around these pockets of progress wherever your timetable allows.

The month begins with the Earth celebrations of Imbolc in the northern hemisphere and Lammas in the southern hemisphere on the 1st, both festivals of fertility that recognize turning points of potential with a desire to honor what we have right now whilst understanding the value of investing in future prosperity.

The Full Moon in Leo on February 5th/6th invites you to align your ambitions with a vision of wholeness, not only with your fellow human beings, but in celebration of your inter-connectedness with the entire web of life! This is a Moon that invites balance and harmony and the Lunar energy at this time may well illuminate any areas of discord, inviting you to take forward thinking measures aimed to restore balance in the here and now and as an investment for future generations to come.

The Super New Moon in Pisces on February 19th/20th supports this wholeheartedly, bringing an incredible day of positive flowing Lunar energy that is primed to support any manifestations that that connect with purpose, calling, and a higher vision.

Our Cards this month of Bless your Past, and Open Yourself to Possibility, combined with Nauthiz, the Rune of Constraint, and Kano the Rune of Openings, invite you to be pro-active whilst simultaneously reflective in releasing any residue of unhelpful past experiences and open yourself to possibility. Be meticulous and pay attention to the details knowing that what you invest in now is building the foundation of your future.

Cards and Runes February 2023

When Nauthiz the Rune of Constraint shows up, it invites you to understand the relationship between your inner and your outer reality and combined with the card of Bless your Past, suggests that any residue of history that is still lingering needs to be reframed so it no longer carries any emotional weight from within.

Additional messages and guidance.
Difficult experiences leave their mark! And whilst physical scars will heal, it is the emotional ones that remain, often resurfacing in the form of repetitive memories and thinking patterns that are laden with powerful emotions, such as fear, anger, resentment, or guilt.

If we continue to go over a past event again and again within our mind, we are fueling the emotional resonance of that event, causing it to continue to cling to us, holding us back and potentially sabotaging our growth and our ability to move forwards in the present time.

Cards and Runes February 2023

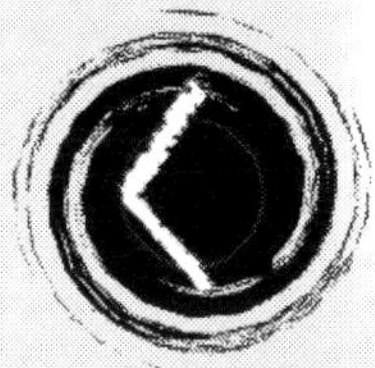

Kano the Rune of Openings shows up for a second month in a row and indicates a time of renewed clarity and significant personal empowerment. Alongside the Card of Open Yourself to Possibility this indicates a time when potential shifts may occur, opening doorways of opportunity for you.

Additional messages and guidance.
Is your vision clouded by self-doubt? Do you lack faith in your abilities? Do you suffer from a lack of confidence that holds you back when opportunities are presented to you?

To be available to receive opportunities from the universe we must first align ourselves with possibility. Every day we face a multitude of choices and decisions, each of which is shaping the future of our tomorrow.

This card asks you to remove any perceptions or attitudes that cloud your vision and hold you back from being open to the infinite source of possibility that the universe wishes for you.

Moon Phases February 2023

The Waxing Gibbous Moon – from January 29th – February 4th passing through Taurus, Gemini, Cancer, and into Leo.

For the best part of this Moon phase the energy gates are open, however, as the Waxing Moon is building in strength, from the 3rd February the overall astro-dynamics do begin to heat up with some significant spikes of Lunar energy coming in. So, if your manifestations are gathering momentum then surf the waves and let the surge of energy move you forwards... but if you are facing any form of indecision or uncertainty, then put down your anchor, and let the current of the Universe show you the way.

The Full Moon - February 5th / 6th - 16° 40' Leo.

The theme of this Full Moon is the creation of balance and harmony and the celebration of inter-connectedness, not only with one another as a collective family of human beings, but of our inter-connectedness with the entire web of life! The Lunar influence of this Moon calls you to be pro-active in recognizing any areas of discord, whether personally, locally, or globally, and to take clear- and forward-thinking measures aimed to restore balance not only in the here and now but as an investment for future generations to come. This Moon also promises to illuminate any personal internal thinking patterns and emotional states of being that impact the way that you engage with the world at large. So, in manifestation the influence of this Moon will help you to adjust your own personal energy in ways that will not only magnetize and draw your desires to you, but also benefit the world at large.

Full Moon Global Timings:

Los Angeles, USA	Sun, 5 Feb 2023 at 10:28 PST
New York, USA	Sun, 5 Feb 2023 at 13:28 EST
Reykjavik, Iceland	Sun, 5 Feb 2023 at 18:28 GMT
London, United Kingdom	Sun, 5 Feb 2023 at 18:28 GMT
Paris, France	Sun, 5 Feb 2023 at 19:28 CET
Cape Town, South Africa	Sun, 5 Feb 2023 at 20:28 SAST
Delhi, India	Sun, 5 Feb 2023 at 23:58 IST
Perth, Australia	Mon, 6 Feb 2023 at 02:28 AWST
Tokyo, Japan	Mon, 6 Feb 2023 at 03:28 JST
Sydney, Australia	Mon, 6 Feb 2023 at 05:28 AEDT
Auckland, New Zealand	Mon, 6 Feb 2023 at 07:28 NZDT
Greenwich Mean Time, GMT	Sun, 5 Feb 2023 at 18:28 GMT

The Disseminating or Waning Gibbous Moon – from February 7th – 12th passing through Leo, Virgo, Libra, and into Scorpio.

The overall Lunar influence during this Moon phase suggests renewed motivation that springs from clarity and self-awareness. The flow of energy is consistent and supports steady perseverance. Take a methodical approach and pay attention to details. Although this is a time to move forwards and invest in taking real actions to bring your manifestations into being, this is not a time to cut corners or seek a quick fix. With a steady focus, by the 11th and 12th you may well see sudden opportunities that reinforce and validate your progress.

The Last Quarter Moon – February 13th – Scorpio.

The overall astro-dynamics today are lovely, and the energy supports a solid space of review with constructive actions to consolidate your progress. Interestingly as the day progresses the energy does begin to heat up bringing a sense of pressure to address any underlying issues that may have previously been overlooked, so if something calls to you from the heart, pause and listen! This is a day that invites you to identify the things that really matter to you and make adjustments in your manifestations to prioritize these aspects of your life, the small things as well as the big stuff!

The Balsamic Moon or Waning Crescent Moon – from February 14th – 18th passing through Sagittarius, Capricorn, and into Aquarius.

The astro-dynamics during this Moon phase brings a cycle of energy that highlights your passions and desires, and then shows you any obstacles in your way, with opportunity to put down them down and lay them to rest. You can then then circle back to the focus of your desires, potentially free from hinderance.
This flow of Lunar potential begins on Valentine's Day, so place your truest desires at the top of your list and commit to them. Between the 14th and the 18th the Lunar influence supports, healing, resolution, and expansion in real terms, and then on the 18th the passions of Valentine's Day return with the potential for you to move ahead and manifest your desires into form.

The Super New Moon - February 19th / 20th - 1° 21' Pisces.

The energy of today's New Moon is incredibly positive! A Pisces New Moon naturally invites you to enter a space of dreamtime enhancing any wishes that are attuned with emotional sensitivity, inspired by the imagination, and connected with your Spiritual awareness.

The Sun and Moon also join forces with the structured solid energy of Saturn, so this is an amazing day not only to set wishes, but also to create and commit fully to intentions that connect you with your purpose, your calling, and a higher vision. If you have been experiencing any difficulties around procrastination, perseverance, or any aspect of self-sabotage, this is an amazing Moon to make a personal commitment to yourself to shift beyond these limitations.

New Moon Global Timings:

Los Angeles, USA	Sun, 19 Feb 2023 at 23:05 PST
New York, USA	Mon, 20 Feb 2023 at 02:05 EST
Reykjavik, Iceland	Mon, 20 Feb 2023 at 07:05 GMT
London, United Kingdom	Mon, 20 Feb 2023 at 07:05 GMT
Paris, France	Mon, 20 Feb 2023 at 08:05 CET
Cape Town, South Africa	Mon, 20 Feb 2023 at 09:05 SAST
Delhi, India	Mon, 20 Feb 2023 at 12:35 IST
Perth, Australia	Mon, 20 Feb 2023 at 15:05 AWST
Tokyo, Japan	Mon, 20 Feb 2023 at 16:05 JST
Sydney, Australia	Mon, 20 Feb 2023 at 18:05 AEDT
Auckland, New Zealand	Mon, 20 Feb 2023 at 20:05 NZDT
Greenwich Mean Time, GMT	Mon, 20 Feb 2023 at 07:05 GMT

The Waxing Crescent Moon – from February 21st – 26th passing through Pisces, Aries, and Taurus.

The positivity is still flowing as our beautiful Moon begins a new phase of momentum and the Lunar influence during this period is in itself, yet another little mini cycle of manifestation and the flow is very distinct. It goes like this... A spike of energy fires you up... leading to a dynamic that promotes and supports different ways of thinking and communicating... be aware of unexpected signs, signals and synchronicities and communications that go beyond the obvious... this fuels flow and momentum... leading to expansion of ideas, release, and transformation... leading to an alignment of karmic openings... wow... and breathe!

The First Quarter Moon – February 27th - Gemini.

This is a day when the Lunar flow supports positive evaluation! If ideas, thoughts, and insights flood into your world today, the purpose is to bring you all the information you need to view any situation from all angles and all possible perspectives. Whatever your schedule demands today, try to make some space for conscious reflection. And if you are experiencing any indecision or uncertainty, let the situation unfold, there may well be more information needed before deciding how to proceed.

The Waxing Gibbous Moon – from February 28th into March passing through Gemini.

The building energy of the Waxing Moon brings a pretty steady Lunar flow. Overall, this period promotes consistent growth, the gathering of momentum, and manifestation through persistent and reliable action. So, as we move into March, in your manifestations, be steadfast... and enjoy the journey!

30 Monday
Taurus / VOC / Gemini

31 Tuesday
Gemini

1 Wednesday
Gemini / VOC / Cancer

Lunar Imbolc
Festivals of Imbolc Northern Hemisphere - Lammas Southern Hemisphere

2 Thursday
Cancer

3 Friday
Cancer

Emotional this eve
after my RMA lecture —
feeling not good enough

Journaling and Notes

4 Saturday
Cancer / VOC / Leo

Crashed today – slept in afternoon for 3 hours – Cdnt sleep all night,

Waxing Gibbous Moon Phase Ends

5 Sunday
Leo

Feel better today

Full Moon 16°40' Leo

6 Monday
Leo / VOC / Virgo

St Brigid's day
Waitangi Day Holiday - NZ
Full Moon 16°40' Leo

7 Tuesday
Virgo

Waning Gibbous Moon Phase Begins

8 Wednesday
Virgo

9 Thursday
Virgo / VOC / Libra

10 Friday
Libra

Journaling and Notes

11 **Saturday**
Libra / VOC / Scorpio

12 **Sunday**
Scorpio

Waning Gibbous Moon Phase Ends

13 **Monday**
Scorpio / VOC

Last Quarter Moon Scorpio

14 **Tuesday**
VOC / Sagittarius

Valentine's Day
Waning Crescent Moon Phase Begins

15 **Wednesday**
Sagittarius

16 **Thursday**
Sagittarius / VOC / Capricorn

Body not right.
aches & pains — liver stuff.

17 **Friday**
Capricorn

Journaling and Notes

18 **Saturday**
Capricorn / VOC / Aquarius

Waning Crescent Moon Phase Ends
Sun Enters Pisces

19 **Sunday**
Aquarius

Super New Moon 1°21' Pisces

20 Monday
Aquarius / VOC / Pisces

Presidents Day - USA
Super New Moon 1°21' Pisces

21 Tuesday
Pisces

V. emotional - not good enough on way home from dreams group - no meetings today (MC / DMC)
Cried at home - feel better at 7pm.

Waxing Crescent Moon Phase Begins

22 Wednesday
Pisces / VOC / Aries

23 Thursday
Aries

24 Friday
Aries / VOC / Taurus

Journaling and Notes

25 **Saturday**

Taurus

26 **Sunday**

Taurus / VOC / Gemini

Waxing Crescent Moon Phase Ends

Desires, Goals, and Intentions for March 2023

Welcome to March 2023

March 2023. Progress and Manifestation. The Fire builds in intensity!

This is certainly an interesting month with the Moon adding her influence and energy to some significant planetary alignments. With the Sun moving into Aries on the 20th heralding the beginning of a new astrological year, and the turning point of the Spring Equinox in the northern hemisphere and the Autumn Equinox in the southern hemisphere, in our manifestations this is a month of potential preparation with many dynamic opportunities to seek spiritual guidance as to the next steps on our pathways of manifestation. Passions and desires may be highlighted, alongside any frustrations with the potential for both movement and stuckness... but all leading to greater clarity and emergence!

The Full Moon in Virgo on the 7th / 8th calls us to wake up and take action and with the New Moon in Aries on the 21st / 22nd setting the pace for new beginnings, the month of March looks to be lively with much potential for inspiration, though this may not necessarily arrive in the form that we were expecting.

The push and pull of the Lunar energy this month is strong, and like waves on the shore, although some will be gentle and steady, every now and then an unexpectedly large wave can roll in and catch us by surprise, so in the overall flow of the month, try not to react or rush into anything.

Tidy up loose ends, be steady in your endeavors and trust that the universe ultimately holds the keys to your success.

Our cards of Take your Time and Opportunity couldn't have said it better and aligning with Berkana, the Rune of Growth, and Jera the Rune of Harvest, we are assured that clarity will come, and a new dawn will emerge.

Berkana the Rune of Growth heralds a new phase in life, and a point of new beginnings with incredible potential, whilst taking care to move ahead with deliberate intent. The card of Take Your Time validates this energetic beautifully, asking you to get present and be responsive to opportunities as they arrive in your world, being sure to reflect along the way to ensure right action.

Additional messages and guidance.
Do not rush!

A certain amount of pressure can be good for us, helping to motivate us and to give us traction, however inappropriate levels of pressure simply add stress to a situation, coloring our decision-making abilities in a shroud of fog, worry and anxiety.

This card asks you to take your time. Whatever your situation, you are asked to get still, remove all aspects of pressure, and make sure that you find genuine clarity before responding to this situation.

Cards and Runes March 2023

Jera the Rune of Harvest indicates beneficial outcomes, but also acknowledges that there is work to be done before the harvest comes to fruition, combined with the card of Opportunity this combination honors the turning point of the Equinox and the point of opportunity that is associated with these festivals of fertility.

Additional messages and guidance.
Opportunities come in many different shapes and sizes, and not always as we expect.

You are also asked to be particularly alert to opportunities that may come in some sort of disguise. For example, if you are experiencing a loss, however painful this may be, every loss marks the opportunity for a new beginning. Likewise, if you are in a challenging situation that appears to be forcing your hand, consider that however uncomfortable you may feel, a doorway of opportunity is being opened for you.

Trust and believe.

Moon Phases March 2023

The Waxing Gibbous Moon – from February 28th – March 6th passing through Gemini, Cancer, Leo, and into Virgo.

The Lunar flow during this Moon phase is pretty steady with a surge of added expansion and vitality coning in on the 2nd of March. Overall, this period promotes consistent growth, the gathering of momentum, and manifestation through persistent and reliable action.
Honor your commitment to your desires… be steadfast… take pleasure in the journey… and enjoy!

The Full Moon - March 7th / 8th - 16° 40' Virgo.

Be prepared for a great awakening!

The energy of this Full Moon is wants us to wake up, see things through new eyes, find higher minded solutions… and then take action to make them real and bring them into form. Now… if anything emerges at this time that requires change, and you happen to have a raging inner critic, then please do not pick yourself (or indeed anyone else) to pieces. This is truly a Moon of powerful potential in our manifestations, inviting change through awareness, so whatever is uppermost in your world invest with integrity, pay attention to the details, do the work and trust that the right doorways are going to open!

Full Moon Global Timings:

Los Angeles, USA	Tue, 7 Mar 2023 at 04:40 PST
New York, USA	Tue, 7 Mar 2023 at 07:40 EST
Reykjavik, Iceland	Tue, 7 Mar 2023 at 12:40 GMT
London, United Kingdom	Tue, 7 Mar 2023 at 12:40 GMT
Paris, France	Tue, 7 Mar 2023 at 13:40 CET
Cape Town, South Africa	Tue, 7 Mar 2023 at 14:40 SAST
Delhi, India	Tue, 7 Mar 2023 at 18:10 IST
Perth, Australia	Tue, 7 Mar 2023 at 20:40 AWST
Tokyo, Japan	Tue, 7 Mar 2023 at 21:40 JST
Sydney, Australia	Tue, 7 Mar 2023 at 23:40 AEDT
Auckland, New Zealand	Wed, 8 Mar 2023 at 01:40 NZDT
Greenwich Mean Time, GMT	Tue, 7 Mar 2023 at 12:40 GMT

The Disseminating or Waning Gibbous Moon – from March 9th – 14th passing through Virgo, Libra, Scorpio and into Sagittarius.

We begin this phase of the Moon with an intense mix of Fire and Water. This powerful collaboration may fire you up, bringing steamy passion and momentum, but any areas of stuckness or indecision could build frustration with lots of energy and nowhere to put it! This energetic breaks open on the 10th and we get space to breath. Overall, even though the Lunar energy is diminishing, the dynamics of this period bring quite a roller coaster of lunar ups and downs... so navigate with awareness, ride the waves, and when in deep water, become a diver!

The Last Quarter Moon – March 15th – Sagittarius.

Depending on your various manifestations and the uniqueness of your personal circumstances, this Last Quarter Moon could feel very creative and absolutely blasting with ideas, possibilities, and potential, or uncomfortably fiery to put it mildly. However this finds you, there is a purpose to this! The Last Quarter Moon naturally invites evaluation, often calling us to let go and lay to rest anything that is hindering our progress and the overall astro-dynamics today are primed for Spiritual guidance so get still, meditate, and listen... you may well be called to adjust, or to accept or forgive. The energy is primed for healing and regeneration.

The Balsamic Moon or Waning Crescent Moon – from March 16th – 20th passing through Capricorn, Aquarius and into Pisces.

The astro-dynamics during this Moon Phase can be almost divided into two segments, with a shift taking place midway on the 18th. During the first part of this Moon phase there are some fairly intense astro-dynamics happening. Curiously enough, the Lunar energy actually runs alongside these intense surges of energy supporting transformation and the establishment of new ways of thinking, seeing, and doing. So, take it steady and when the shift occurs midway, move forwards gently and practice the art of allowing as we move towards the New Moon and a space of new openings and possibilities.

The New Moon - March 21st / 22nd - 0° 48' Aries.

The Sun entering Aries marks the beginning of a new astrological year which combined with the Spring Equinox in the northern hemisphere and the Autumn Equinox in the southern hemisphere really do make this a New Moon of new beginnings.

Just before the Moon and Sun meet we see a surge of fiery energy igniting the Lunar pathway with the planets aligning to bring optimum creativity, with opportunity to heal, collaborate, and view life through the eyes of love.

The overall dynamics of the day offer powerful levels of karmic healing and this Moon invites us to send requests into the universe in the form of prayers wishes and intentions, that we may find new hope and optimism. If you meditate regularly you may wish to extend your meditation period today with a clear intent to receive the guidance and support that you need at this time, and if you are new to meditation, this is an amazing day to get started!

New Moon Global Timings:

Los Angeles, USA	Tue, 21 Mar 2023 at 10:22 PDT
New York, USA	Tue, 21 Mar 2023 at 13:22 EDT
Reykjavik, Iceland	Tue, 21 Mar 2023 at 17:22 GMT
London, United Kingdom	Tue, 21 Mar 2023 at 17:22 GMT
Paris, France	Tue, 21 Mar 2023 at 18:22 CET
Cape Town, South Africa	Tue, 21 Mar 2023 at 19:22 SAST
Delhi, India	Tue, 21 Mar 2023 at 22:52 IST
Perth, Australia	Wed, 22 Mar 2023 at 01:22 AWST
Tokyo, Japan	Wed, 22 Mar 2023 at 02:22 JST
Sydney, Australia	Wed, 22 Mar 2023 at 04:22 AEDT
Auckland, New Zealand	Wed, 22 Mar 2023 at 06:22 NZDT
Greenwich Mean Time, GMT	Tue, 21 Mar 2023 at 17:22 GMT

The Waxing Crescent Moon – from March 23rd – 27th passing through Aries, Taurus, and Gemini.

Perseverance and consistency are key words during this phase of the Moon. We see particularly strong spikes of Lunar influence on both the 24th and the 26th but these are fleeting and may well add traction to your emerging projects and growth or highlight areas that require evaluation to continue successfully. The overall energy suggests a steady flow of emergence with growing potential.

The First Quarter Moon – March 28th / 29th - Cancer.

The first quarter Moon is in nurturing Cancer and the overall astrodynamics offer impetus and the energy to move things forward. This third Moon cycle of the year naturally invites us to weigh things up, see the truth of any situation so we may make appropriate decisions and navigate with greater awareness. So take time to listen, notice, and consider, and pay particular attention to any signs and synchronicities that reveal themselves to you.

The Waxing Gibbous Moon – from March 30th into April passing through Cancer into Leo.

This Moon phase begins with a strong call for healing so listen up and attend to whatever is needed. The last two days of March see a distinct shift in the Lunar energy inviting flow and re-birth. As we move into April unexpected opportunities may well be calling.

27 **Monday**
Gemini

First Quarter Moon Gemini

28 **Tuesday**
Gemini

Waxing Gibbous Moon Phase Begins

1 **Wednesday**
Gemini / VOC / Cancer

2 **Thursday**
Cancer

3 **Friday**
Cancer / VOC / Leo

Journaling and Notes

4 Saturday
Leo

A lot of pain in lower back & Hips when I woke up - not sure if this is food related - I ate eggs & sour dough bugette on Thurs / Fri.

5 Sunday
Leo

↓ same today - I rubbed some Hemp cream & felt some swelling in lower back - so I've done something - but not sure. Paracetmol today.

6 Monday
Leo / VOC / Virgo

Back & hips easing but still not right.

Waxing Gibbous Moon Phase Ends

7 Tuesday
Virgo

Soca stuff came up at MC – v. difficult to discuss. Susie v. resistant & I & Alice were both not heard.

Full Moon 16°40' Virgo

8 Wednesday
Virgo / VOC / Libra

Full Moon 16°40' Virgo

9 Thursday
Libra

Went to Tesco & got some food – eve – felt I picked "a bug up"

Waning Gibbous Moon Phase Begins

10 Friday
Libra/ VOC

Not feeling great lots of sneezing not sure if cold or Hay fever

Journaling and Notes

11 Saturday
VOC / Scorpio

Totally knackered
in & out
of a cold.

12 Sunday
Scorpio

13 Monday
Scorpio / VOC / Sagittarius

Still not feeling great,

14 Tuesday
Sagittarius

Waning Gibbous Moon Phase Ends

15 Wednesday
Sagittarius / VOC / Capricorn

Still not great

Last Quarter Moon Sagittarius

16 Thursday
Capricorn

Cancelled clients today

Waning Crescent Moon Phase Begins

17 Friday
Capricorn / VOC / Aquarius

+ today

Saint Patrick's Day

Journaling and Notes

lost voice on Friday – not well – laryngitis – had to cancel w/end. Also cancelled dreams group for 21st March & clients on Monday 20th – I spoke with Andrea yesterday & it is exactly 3 yrs ago on 23rd March that 1st lockdown happened. I wonder whether this is why I am ill, Also been waking up over 18/19 at 3.15am V. emotional & also feeling emotional for whole week.

18 **Saturday**
Aquarius

/ Cancelled
ill.
2nd Dreams
w/end.

19 **Sunday**
Aquarius / VOC / Pisces

UK Mother's Day

20 **Monday** Concelled Clients

Pisces

Spring Equinox Northern Hemisphere – Autumn Equinox Southern Hemisphere
Sun Enters Aries
Waning Crescent Moon Phase Ends

21 **Tuesday** Cancelled dreams group & ~~[illegible]~~ MC

Pisces / VOC / Aries

New Moon 0°48' Aries – 17:22

22 **Wednesday**

Aries

New Moon 0°48' Aries

23 **Thursday**

Aries / VOC / Taurus

Waxing Crescent Moon Phase Begins

24 **Friday** 2 wks still not well

Taurus

Journaling and Notes

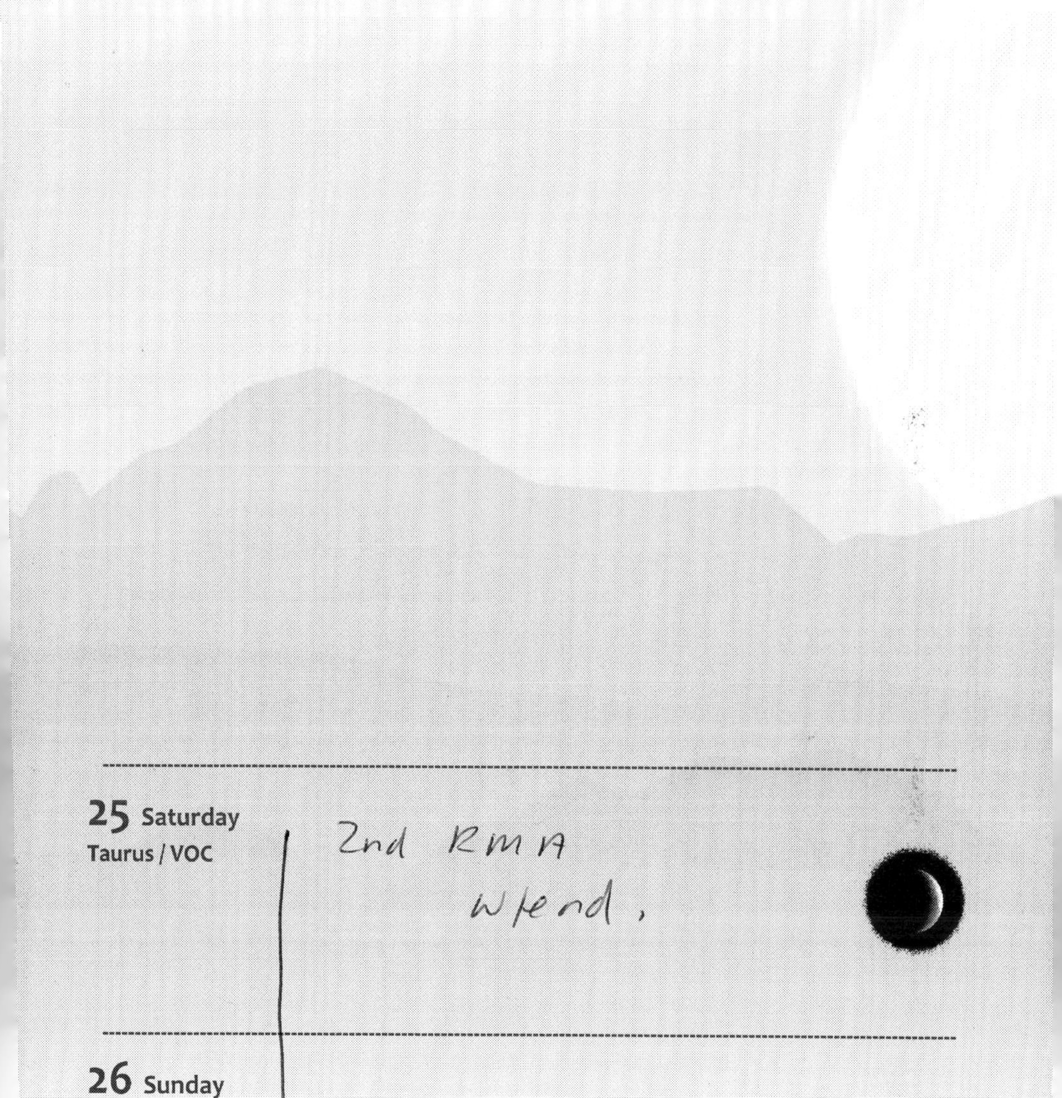

25 **Saturday**
Taurus / VOC

2nd RMA
wkend,

26 **Sunday**
VOC / Gemini

UK Clocks Change

27 Monday
Gemini

Waxing Crescent Moon Phase Ends

28 Tuesday
Gemini / VOC / Cancer

First Quarter Moon Cancer

29 Wednesday
Cancer

First Quarter Moon Cancer

30 Thursday
Cancer / VOC / Leo

Waxing Gibbous Moon Phase Begins

31 Friday
Leo

Journaling and Notes

1 Saturday
Leo

Still not
well
bad week

2 Sunday
Leo / VOC / Virgo

Sinus pain,
blocked ears

Desires, Goals, and Intentions for April 2023

Welcome to April 2023

April 2023. A Month of Movement.

April looks to be a month of movement and significant progression… a kind of assessment… review… and then full steam ahead!

The Full Moon in Libra on the 5th / 6th is absolutely loaded with possibility and potential with liberation and newfound freedoms that emerge through the karmic healing of old wounds, including those that have been passed down through generations!

In preparation for the New Moon on the 19th / 20th which also heralds the beginning of eclipse season, the energy is remarkably busy this month with surges of heightened awareness rushing in to keep you on your toes.

With Mercury moving into retrograde on the 21st we might expect some delays and interruptions, but given the overall flow of energy, we can be sure that any disruptions are serving a purpose and bringing important information to the fore. This is definitely not a month to sit back and take it easy, although there are some days when stillness and dreaming will pay dividends in finding clarity of vision and seeing what is needed and when to take action.

So, in alignment with the insight offered by our cards of Choices and Decisions with Ansuz the Rune of Signals, and the card of the Spiritual Warrior, aligning with Fehu, the Rune of Possessions, pace yourself and be pro-active whilst also simultaneously steady enough to be present and in the moment. This way, you can observe and engage with every experience as a sign bringing windows of opportunity to fast forward your manifestations.

Ansuz the Rune of Signals aligns beautifully with the energy of Eclipse season plus the influence of Mercury in retrograde when we are called to recognize that even a delay or disruption may be providential. In collaboration with the card of Choices and Decisions we are urged to make choices without fear and always be responsive in the here and now.

Additional messages and guidance.

Do you overburden yourself in the process of making decisions, creating an internal stream of challenging thoughts that try to anticipate every potential outcome, for fear of making the wrong choice?

In truth, there is no such thing as a wrong choice or a wrong decision. None of us can actually know how something will be until we get there and try it on for size! This is how we learn. This is how we grow. And it is through this learning process that we discover the things that work for us, as well as the things that do not, helping us to find clarity in our future decisions and choices.

Fehu, the Rune of Possessions speaks of fulfillment and ambitions satisfied, calling for internal enquiry to be clear about what truly matters to you. Aligning with the card of the Spiritual Warrior be alert to your inner world and inner calling over and above any external gains and successes.

Additional messages and guidance.
Sometimes this card indicates a series of events/circumstances/situations that have created a gradual awakening within you, causing you to question your current circumstances. Sometimes it can indicate a sudden, out of your control event, that has pushed you to have to make decisions and change course or you may have been feeling restless and as if something needs to change. Perhaps you are already in the process of a major transition in your life and wondering if you have taken the right direction.

Whatever your situation, this card is an affirmation. You are invited to listen to your circumstances as a form of guidance.

You are aligning with the calling of your Soul. This is the pathway of the Spiritual Warrior.

Moon Phases April 2023

The Waxing Gibbous Moon – from March 30th - April 4th passing through Cancer, Leo, Virgo and into Libra.

This Moon phase begins with a strong call for healing so listen up and attend to whatever is needed. The last two days of March see a distinct shift in the Lunar energy inviting flow and re-birth. As we move into April the Lunar flow is on the up and actively promotes and supports the emergence of new ways of seeing, being, and doing! So, if any hold ups show up in your world or you experience any waves of self-doubt, particularly around the 2nd and 4th then step back, observe, and review, and use this information to bring you a greater clarity of direction… and then invest fully!

The Full Moon – April 5th / 6th - 16° 07' Libra.

This is a Full Moon that says… Let's make it happen! And the overall astro-dynamics are aligning to support a seriously big attitude of possibility!

A Libra Full Moon will always be calling for balance and harmony and this particular Moon favors healing, forgiveness, the release of the past, with a real sense of liberation, and in particular, freedom of expression. So have your voice and dare to believe in possibility… the energy supports growth and emergence in a big way today!

Full Moon Global Timings:

Los Angeles, USA	Wed, 5 Apr 2023 at 21:34 PDT
New York, USA	Thu, 6 Apr 2023 at 00:34 EDT
Reykjavik, Iceland	Thu, 6 Apr 2023 at 04:34 GMT
London, United Kingdom	Thu, 6 Apr 2023 at 05:34 BST
Paris, France	Thu, 6 Apr 2023 at 06:34 CEST
Cape Town, South Africa	Thu, 6 Apr 2023 at 06:34 SAST
Delhi, India	Thu, 6 Apr 2023 at 10:04 IST
Perth, Australia	Thu, 6 Apr 2023 at 12:34 AWST
Tokyo, Japan	Thu, 6 Apr 2023 at 13:34 JST
Sydney, Australia	Thu, 6 Apr 2023 at 14:34 AEST
Auckland, New Zealand	Thu, 6 Apr 2023 at 16:34 NZST
Greenwich Mean Time, GMT	Thu, 6 Apr 2023 at 04:34 GMT

The Disseminating or Waning Gibbous Moon – from April 7th – 12th passing through Scorpio, Sagittarius and into Capricorn.

Heightened levels of communication dominate the Lunar flow for the first couple of days into this Moon phase, bringing opportunity to process at depth the powerful emergence of new possibilities shown at the Full Moon. As the Moon passes through Sagittarius and into Capricorn the Lunar energy supports investment and positive progress resulting in steady solid results. So be consistent and steadfast... as we come to the end of this phase, the Lunar connections suggest a consolidation of existing plans alongside the clear formulation of new ideas, bringing renewed clarity of direction in all areas.

The Last Quarter Moon April 13th – Capricorn.

This Last Quarter Moon has a very fast pace about it with changeable connections throughout the day. Depending on the age and stage of your various manifestations, I would try to maintain a balance of pausing to review, whilst also surfing the waves and seizing the moment! For anything that is flowing forwards then go with it and enjoy the buzz of this busy energy... but if anything jolts or doesn't feel quite right for you, just put the brakes on, take note, listen, and observe, the learning will most likely relate to some aspect of your world that isn't quite in balance.

The Balsamic Moon or Waning Crescent Moon – from April 14th – 18th passing through Aquarius, Pisces and into Aries.

The overall flavor of this phase is all about movement and progress... however, with Mercury now in retrograde, even though there is an intensity in the Lunar influence around the 14th and 15th the Lunar flow then steadies into a gentler pace offering a space of calm availability. And this is purposeful, asking you to achieve progress, not through rushing, but through conscious, thought through actions. And there is a delightful window of opportunity just before the New Moon on the 20th to really slow down and create beautifully crafted wishes and intentions that align your desires and manifestations with a legacy worthy of future generations.

The New Moon Eclipse – April 19th / 20th - 29° 49' Aries.

This New Moon at 29° 49' Aries is literally on the cusp of Aries and Taurus and so we can use this shift in energy from the Aries influence of new beginnings into steady solid earthy Taurus, to bring our manifestations into form.

Added to this we have an incredibly powerful set of astro-dynamics that hold profound karmic potential... and it's eclipse season!

So... what are the changes that you wish to see in the world? Dream big and infuse your wishes with your highest possible vision of the future! And now set intentions that commit you to doing and being your absolute personal best, literally inviting the universe to support you in living in alignment with all that you wish to see in the world!

New Moon

Los Angeles, USA	Wed, 19 Apr 2023 at 21:12 PDT
New York, USA	Thu, 20 Apr 2023 at 00:12 EDT
Reykjavik, Iceland	Thu, 20 Apr 2023 at 04:12 GMT
London, United Kingdom	Thu, 20 Apr 2023 at 05:12 BST
Paris, France	Thu, 20 Apr 2023 at 06:12 CEST
Cape Town, South Africa	Thu, 20 Apr 2023 at 06:12 SAST
Delhi, India	Thu, 20 Apr 2023 at 09:42 IST
Perth, Australia	Thu, 20 Apr 2023 at 12:12 AWST
Tokyo, Japan	Thu, 20 Apr 2023 at 13:12 JST
Sydney, Australia	Thu, 20 Apr 2023 at 14:12 AEST
Auckland, New Zealand	Thu, 20 Apr 2023 at 16:12 NZST
Greenwich Mean Time, GMT	Thu, 20 Apr 2023 at 04:12 GMT

The Waxing Crescent Moon – from April 21st – 26th passing through Taurus, Gemini and into Cancer.

Overall, there is a super nice flow of Lunar energy during this Moon phase bringing a fairly steady get up and go influence, although the pace does look to speed up a bit just before the next moon phase of the first quarter. If you find yourself feeling a bit dreamy around the 24th then lean into this space of possibility... sometimes progress comes through stillness rather than action and you may well find that time out or time still will give you exactly what you need to bring clarity.

The First Quarter Moon – April 27th / 28th - Leo.

The astro-dynamics of this first quarter Moon are powerful, dynamic, and forthright, asking you to listen up... there is a distinct feel of karmic happenings, with meetings, circumstances and situations that feel as though they are guided by fate or destiny. So take heed of any signs signals and synchronicities and take them seriously.

The Waxing Gibbous Moon – from April 29th into May passing through Leo into Virgo.

We are now in full on Eclipse season and the lunar energy is rising so this Moon phase is absolutely primed for acceleration and as we move into May the energy will promote circumstances that can move your manifestations forwards, so I would suggest steering the review energy of the first quarter into some productive forward planning and timetabling.

3 Monday
Virgo

4 Tuesday
Virgo / VOC / Libra

Waxing Gibbous Moon Phase Ends

5 Wednesday
Libra

Full Moon 16°07' Libra

6 Thursday
Libra/ VOC

Full Moon 16°07' Libra

7 Friday
VOC / Scorpio

4 wks - still got cough, blocked nose - ears blocked.

Waning Gibbous Moon Phase Begins
Good Friday Bank Holiday UK

Journaling and Notes

8 Saturday

Scorpio

9 Sunday

Scorpio / VOC / Sagittarius

Easter Day

10 Monday
Sagittarius

Easter Monday Bank Holiday UK

11 Tuesday
Sagittarius / VOC / Capricorn

12 Wednesday
Capricorn

Waning Gibbous Moon Phase Ends

13 Thursday
Capricorn / VOC / Aquarius

Last Quarter Moon Capricorn

14 Friday
Aquarius

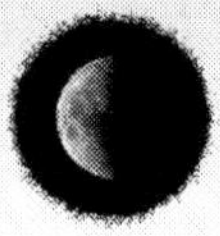

Waning Crescent Moon Phase Begins

Journaling and Notes

15 Saturday
Aquarius / VOC / Pisces

16 Sunday
Pisces

17 Monday
Pisces / VOC

Easter Monday

18 Tuesday
VOC / Aries

Waning Crescent Moon Phase Ends

19 Wednesday
Aries

New Moon Eclipse 29°49’ Aries

20 Thursday
Aries / VOC / Taurus

New Moon Eclipse 29°49’ Aries
Sun Enters Taurus

21 Friday
Taurus

Mercury Retrograde Begins
Waxing Crescent Moon Phase Begins

Journaling and Notes

22 **Saturday**

Taurus / VOC / Gemini

23 **Sunday**

Gemini

24 Monday
Gemini / VOC / Cancer

25 Tuesday
Cancer

26 Wednesday
Cancer / VOC

Waxing Crescent Moon Phase Ends

27 Thursday
VOC / Leo

First Quarter Moon Leo

28 Friday
Leo

First Quarter Moon Leo

Journaling and Notes

29 Saturday
Leo / VOC / Virgo

Waxing Gibbous Moon Phase Begins

30 Sunday
Virgo

Desires, Goals, and Intentions for May 2023

Welcome to May 2023

May 2023. Change is happening... so let's work with it!

If April ended with an overall message of full steam ahead then May is pulling out all of the stops... and in a very interesting way!
We begin the month bang in the middle of Eclipse season which can really heighten the potential for fast paced realizations that create shifts and openings. We also see Mercury in retrograde until the 15th which often heralds interruptions and delays.

Now this can seem like a contradiction in energy flow, but... if you consider the energy of the Mercury retrograde as a call to slow down, look backwards, and see what needs to be done differently, whilst taking actions in the present to create those changes then this collaboration begins to make sense.

The Full Moon in Scorpio on the 5th / 6th promises to illuminate and highlight any areas of your world that need to be brought into balance, whilst also showing you exactly what you need to do to make this happen, and the New Moon on the 19th / 20th not only supports the new, but almost demands change, re-birth, and transformation, so there will be ample opportunity to see exactly what you need to change and the supporting energy to make this real, working from the inside out!

The cards of Intention and Course Correct hold this transformational energy supported by Inguz, the Rune of Fertility and Jera, the Rune of Harvest, highlighting this interesting month of dynamic possibility.

Inguz, the Rune of Fertility asks for completion of beginnings and highlights the need for adjustments to be made at the beginning of any new phase of life and the card of Course Correct beautifully tunes into this theme, particularly when the astro-dynamics are the influenced by a Mercury retrograde period.

Additional messages and guidance.
In our goal driven culture, we so often interpret disruptions, delays, and diversions as a negative experience, creating frustration and leaving us feeling angry or helpless. However, if we change our perspective and trust that the universe is bringing us exactly what we need… exactly when we need it… then we can understand that even a delay or diversion is in fact a gift, bringing us a sign or a communication that we need to make some adjustments, course correct, or even take a completely different direction.

This card is here to reassure you that any delays taking place in your current situation are timely and are simply signposts to assist you in taking the next step in the right direction.

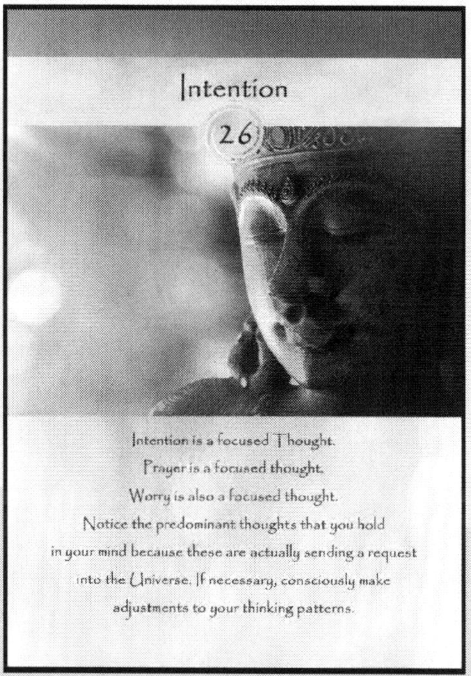

Jera, the Rune of Harvest alongside the card of Intention is a reminder that what you think is creating your future!

Additional messages and guidance.
When we set intentions, we are focusing our thoughts and giving our attention to a direction or a situation that we desire. What we frequently forget is that the universe will respond to our predominant and most focused thoughts, and that outside of the times when we collate our thoughts into focused intention, our mind is still involved in a continual stream of thinking.

If this thinking does not resonate with our core wishes, it can act as a block, getting in the way of the universe delivering us a pathway that will lead to our desires, particularly if the time we spend on our focused intentions is considerably less than the time that our mind is left to run free into more negative thinking patterns. This card asks you to bring your attention to any autopilot thinking patterns that may be limiting or interrupting your intended, focused, intentional thought.

Moon Phases May 2023

The Waxing Gibbous Moon – from April 29th – May 4th passing through Leo, Virgo and into Libra

We are now in full on Eclipse season which often means that things can happen quite quickly… and the lunar energy is rising, and this Moon phase is absolutely primed for acceleration. As you move ahead, planning and timetabling will help you to use the Lunar influence at its absolute best. The overall energy is busy and happening so be thoughtful about pacing yourself as we see some surges of dynamic energy rushing in as we approach the Full Moon Eclipse.

The Full Moon Eclipse – May 5th / 6th - 14° 57' Scorpio.

This is a very dynamic Full Moon with the potential not only to illuminate and highlight any areas of your world that need to be brought into balance, but also to show you exactly what to do to make this happen, and in real terms.

A Full Moon in Scorpio will tend to illuminate the shadows, inviting you to dive deep and look at yourself and your situations with honesty, and this Full Moon is no exception. With the added influence of the Eclipse which is said to create an energetic rift or portal to help you to connect with your purpose and calling in this present lifetime, plus a powerful connection with Uranus, the great awakener, this looks to be an interesting time of light bulb moments and sudden opportunities… so fasten your seatbelt and enjoy the ride!

Full Moon Global Timings:

Los Angeles, USA	Fri, 5 May 2023 at 10:33 PDT
New York, USA	Fri, 5 May 2023 at 13:33 EDT
Reykjavik, Iceland	Fri, 5 May 2023 at 17:33 GMT
London, United Kingdom	Fri, 5 May 2023 at 18:33 BST
Paris, France	Fri, 5 May 2023 at 19:33 CEST
Cape Town, South Africa	Fri, 5 May 2023 at 19:33 SAST
Delhi, India	Fri, 5 May 2023 at 23:03 IST
Perth, Australia	Sat, 6 May 2023 at 01:33 AWST
Tokyo, Japan	Sat, 6 May 2023 at 02:33 JST
Sydney, Australia	Sat, 6 May 2023 at 03:33 AEST
Auckland, New Zealand	Sat, 6 May 2023 at 05:33 NZST
Greenwich Mean Time, GMT	Fri, 5 May 2023 at 17:33 GMT

The Disseminating or Waning Gibbous Moon – from May 7th – 11th passing through Scorpio, Sagittarius, Capricorn and into Aquarius.

The Lunar influence is flowing incredibly well throughout this Moon phase with an emphasis on moving ahead through conscious heightened awareness, so pay particular attention to any sign's, signals, and synchronicities… the way will be shown. And with Mercury still in retrograde, opportunities may arrive in unexpected ways. Yes… even delays and interruptions may ultimately prove to be helpful, bringing just the information you need to move steadily forwards… even if it's not immediately obvious!

The Last Quarter Moon May 12th – Aquarius.

This Last Quarter Moon is going to be speaking to you from the heart… so listen well. This energy at this time may well call you to change your perception or perspectives on some aspect of your world, bringing you the empowerment that to become the creator of any changes that you wish to manifest in your world. Expect the unexpected and be open to all that happens.

The Balsamic Moon or Waning Crescent Moon – from May 13th – 18th passing through Pisces, Aries and into Taurus.

The start of this Moon Phase feels very Karmic, full of potential openings, and very much aligned with the flavor of fate and destiny… and in the most positive way! It feels like one of those periods when things can just fall into place and the universe has your back. However, the Lunar energy intensifies significantly on the 17th / 18th so be anchored and take small steps rather than rushing ahead. Slow and steady wins the race!

The New Moon – May 19th / 20th - 28° 25' Taurus.

This is a New Moon that doesn't just support the new… the Lunar energy is not just calling, but almost demanding, re-birth and transformation! So get to it and harness this incredible energy to enhance your wishes and intentions.

This is an amazing New Moon to let go of any insecurities or unhelpful habits that have previously held you back and commit fully to a new pro-active approach that takes you out of your safe zone and into your stretch zone, building your confidence slowly and steadily.

Let the universe open some doors for you… then dare to step through them!

New Moon Global Timings:

Los Angeles, USA	Fri, 19 May 2023 at 08:53 PDT
New York, USA	Fri, 19 May 2023 at 11:53 EDT
Reykjavik, Iceland	Fri, 19 May 2023 at 15:53 GMT
London, United Kingdom	Fri, 19 May 2023 at 16:53 BST
Paris, France	Fri, 19 May 2023 at 17:53 CEST
Cape Town, South Africa	Fri, 19 May 2023 at 17:53 SAST
Delhi, India	Fri, 19 May 2023 at 21:23 IST
Perth, Australia	Fri, 19 May 2023 at 23:53 AWST
Tokyo, Japan	Sat, 20 May 2023 at 00:53 JST
Sydney, Australia	Sat, 20 May 2023 at 01:53 AEST
Auckland, New Zealand	Sat, 20 May 2023 at 03:53 NZST
Greenwich Mean Time, GMT	Fri, 19 May 2023 at 15:53 GMT

The Waxing Crescent Moon – from May 21st – 26th passing through Gemini, Cancer and into Leo.

Sometimes a Waxing Crescent Moon phase can bring a gentle steady forward motion…but not this one, the flow of Lunar energy is pretty strong from the get-go… and increases in acceleration!

In the overall astro-dynamics there is a distinctly Karmic flavor in the ethers, so be aware of potential openings especially on the 22nd.

As the Moon journeys through emotional Cancer and into Leo we see some significantly intense dynamics that support action and forward motion!

The First Quarter Moon – May 27th Virgo.

The first quarter Moon is naturally a time of review and evaluation, and the Lunar influence of this particular quarter Moon is absolutely primed to assist you in building new structures and solid foundations for your future manifestations.

This is a great day to make lists and plan ahead, focusing on the steps that you can take, right here and right now.

If the overall rapid flow of energy has been pushing you forwards this is also the perfect time to do a check in, crossing the T's and dotting the I's to ensure that in the overall fast-moving energetics you are paying attention to the details.

The Waxing Gibbous Moon – from May 28th into June passing through Virgo into Libra.

The start of this Moon phase places an emphasis on communication and collaboration to assist productivity. We begin to see a shift in the energy on 29th as the Moon builds in intensity towards the coming Full Moon. If you struggle with any form of self-doubt then rather than wobble... reach out for help and talk about it.

May 2023

1 Monday
Virgo / VOC

Pluto Retrograde Begins
Festival of Beltane Northern Hemisphere – Samhain Southern Hemisphere
UK Early May Bank Holiday

2 Tuesday
VOC / Libra

3 Wednesday
Libra

4 Thursday
Libra / VOC / Scorpio

Waxing Gibbous Moon Ends

5 Friday
Scorpio

Full Moon Eclipse 14°57’ Scorpio

Journaling and Notes

6 Saturday
Scorpio / VOC / Sagittarius

Full Moon Eclipse $14^\circ 57'$ Scorpio

7 Sunday
Sagittarius

Waning Gibbous Moon Phase Begins

8 Monday
Sagittarius / VOC / Capricorn

9 Tuesday
Capricorn

10 Wednesday
Capricorn / VOC

11 Thursday
VOC / Aquarius

Waning Gibbous Moon Phase Ends

12 Friday
Aquarius

Last Quarter Moon Aquarius

Journaling and Notes

13 Saturday

Aquarius / VOC / Pisces

Waning Crescent Moon Phase Begins

14 Sunday

Pisces

USA, Canada, Australia & New Zealand Mother's Day

15 **Monday**
Pisces / VOC / Aries

Mercury Retrograde Ends

16 **Tuesday**
Aries

17 **Wednesday**
Aries / VOC / Taurus

18 **Thursday**
Taurus

Waning Crescent Moon Phase Ends

19 **Friday**
Taurus / VOC / Gemini

New Moon 28°25’ Taurus

Journaling and Notes

---

20 **Saturday**

Gemini

New Moon 28°25' Taurus

---

21 **Sunday**

Gemini / VOC

Waxing Crescent Moon Phase Begins
Sun Enters Gemini

---

22 **Monday**
VOC / Cancer

23 **Tuesday**
Cancer

24 **Wednesday**
Cancer / VOC / Leo

25 **Thursday**
Leo

26 **Friday**
Leo / VOC

Waxing Crescent Moon Phase Ends

Journaling and Notes

27 **Saturday**
VOC / Virgo

First Quarter Moon Virgo

28 **Sunday**
Virgo

Waxing Gibbous Moon Phase Begins

Desires, Goals, and Intentions for June 2023

Welcome to June 2023

June 2023. Busy... transformational... and potentially very productive!

June looks to be a pretty busy month with a ton of opportunities to feel our way into the new, whilst holding a clarity of mind at the same time.

There are definitely some ups and downs and moments of upheaval, however despite this, the Lunar influence looks to soften the impact by bringing an underlying feeling of positivity calling for renewed hope and a shift in mindset to imagine the very real possibility of a brighter future.

Yes there is work to do to make this real, and with the great teacher Saturn, moving into retrograde on the 17th, wholeheartedly supporting the letting go of old structures and systems that no longer serve, this is a month when the pathway ahead may become clearer in terms of your own unique contribution to bring about the lasting and significant, much needed changes, that humanity and the world at large is crying out for... though this clarity may arrive in unexpected ways!

As the new emerges this will inevitable involve some the letting go of the past. The Full Moon in Sagittarius on the 3rd and 4th is particularly supportive of renewed faith and trust with openings that suggest justice, healing, and resolution whilst the New Moon in Gemini on the 17th and 18th feels very motivated with a profoundly spiritual flavor.

The card of Grace, with Hagalaz the Rune of Disruption, followed by the card of Trust the Universe, and Jera, the Rune of Harvest, showing up for the third time this year, bring exactly the advice and guidance we need to navigate this month to our fullest potential.

Cards and Runes June 2023

Hagalaz the Rune of Disruption calls for freedom and liberation from any aspects of your world that no longer serve, and the card of Grace invites you to approach the need for change through the eyes of compassion and understanding, whether to yourself, or to others.

Additional messages and guidance.

Grace is that extraordinary voice within us that supports us in approaching all aspects of our lives with harmony, balance, love, and kindness, always desiring to give the very best of ourselves in any situation, even if we find ourselves in a conflictual situation or needing to do something that we would perhaps rather not do.

When Grace flows through us, love becomes the focus of all of our thoughts, words, and actions, radiating out into the world, positively affecting everyone and everything we come into contact with. If this card is drawn in response to a challenging situation or person, you are asked to stand back and review your situation through the eyes of grace. Now take action accordingly.

Cards and Runes June 2023

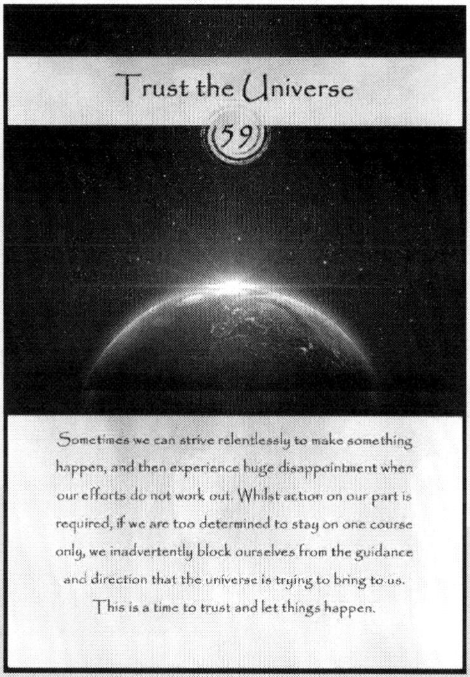

Jera, the Rune of Harvest shows up for a second month in a row, indicating that investments to build a real and lasting sustainable future are fully supported, and in alignment with the card of Trust the Universe, you are assured that in this month of potential, the Universe will always hold the highest possible vision for you.

Additional messages and guidance.
Do you have a very fixed direction in your mind that you believe will help you to achieve your vision and your goals in the most efficient and speediest way? This card is a reminder, that sometimes an alternative course of action, whilst taking a little longer, may in fact be the best way forwards, providing additional information and the opportunity to develop new skills along the route. Indeed sometimes, a deviation in our pathway can cause us to course correct or even take an entirely different direction which ultimately supports us in aligning with our greater purpose.

If something is not running smoothly in your life, trust that the universe has a hand in this process and allow things to unfold as they should. Your direction will become clear to you.

Moon Phases June 2023

The Waxing Gibbous Moon – from May 28th - June 2nd passing through Virgo, Libra, Scorpio and into Sagittarius.

The start of this Moon phase places an emphasis on communication and collaboration to assist productivity. We begin to see a shift in the energy on 29th as the Moon builds in intensity towards the coming Full Moon. If you struggle with any form of self-doubt then rather than wobble… the lunar influence invites you to reach out for help and talk about it. As we move into June the overall dynamics intensify and the Moon lends her energy in support of both creating change whilst also helping you to find your way through insight and an awareness of the importance of balance in all things.

And just before the Full Moon we see a significant shift in the Lunar flow highlighting optimism and renewed hope. Fab!

The Full Moon – June 3rd / 4th - 13° 17' Sagittarius.

This beautiful Full Moon in Sagittarius continues the flavor of optimism bringing dynamics that are particularly supportive of opportunity and renewed faith and trust with openings that suggest justice, healing, and resolution.
This is a Moon that promises to highlight the connection between your thoughts and your words and your external reality, bringing ample energy, not only to observe these connections, but to make conscious changes to any internal blocks of negativity that could be hindering your ongoing manifestations. Lean into this energy with passion and vigor, this is one of those moments when the tide promises to carry you in exactly the right direction… with Karmic precision!

Full Moon Global Timings:

Los Angeles, USA	Sat, 3 Jun 2023 at 20:41 PDT
New York, USA	Sat, 3 Jun 2023 at 23:41 EDT
Reykjavik, Iceland	Sun, 4 Jun 2023 at 03:41 GMT
London, United Kingdom	Sun, 4 Jun 2023 at 04:41 BST
Paris, France	Sun, 4 Jun 2023 at 05:41 CEST
Cape Town, South Africa	Sun, 4 Jun 2023 at 05:41 SAST
Delhi, India	Sun, 4 Jun 2023 at 09:11 IST
Perth, Australia	Sun, 4 Jun 2023 at 11:41 AWST
Tokyo, Japan	Sun, 4 Jun 2023 at 12:41 JST
Sydney, Australia	Sun, 4 Jun 2023 at 13:41 AEST
Auckland, New Zealand	Sun, 4 Jun 2023 at 15:41 NZST
Greenwich Mean Time, GMT	Sun, 4 Jun 2023 at 03:41 GMT

The Disseminating or Waning Gibbous Moon – from June 5th – 9th passing through Scorpio, Capricorn, Aquarius and into Pisces.

The overall astrodynamics are fully focused on transformation, re-birth, and emergence and during this phase the Lunar flow feels pretty fast paced with some significant surges of energy… almost as if progress is happening and it's hard to slow anything down or put the brakes on to pause and take stock. So, if anything in your world is feeling a bit all over the place, just go with it and trust… the Universe will be holding the higher purpose.

The Last Quarter Moon June 10th – Pisces.

Given the hectic busyness of June so far, the influence of this Last Quarter Moon promises to bring a bit more groundedness with the purpose of finding clarity. If your schedule affords it, then timetable a decent chunk of time to get still, and really evaluate from the inside out. The Lunar influence suggests the potential to find practical and very realistic solutions and answers.

The Balsamic Moon or Waning Crescent Moon – from June 11th – 17th passing through Pisces, Aries, Taurus, and into Gemini.

Although we see a couple of slightly more intense surges of energy on the 15th and 17th, overall, the Lunar flow during this Moon phase is refreshingly steady counterbalancing some of the more impatient undercurrents in the overall astro-dynamics. Given that the Moon tunes into some beautifully expansive and very Karmic potential, take full advantage of this period to catch your breath and give your full focus to those areas of your world that you want to prioritize and invest in.

The New Moon – June 17th / 18th - 26° 42' Gemini.

The 24 hour build up to this New Moon feels very positive and very motivated creating an ideal pocket of time to set clear wishes and intentions.

The overall energy of the day favors profound spiritual connections, however, if there are any areas of uncertainty or confusion in your life, this could feel a little overwhelming… so set your wishes and intentions but don't rush to make things happen or move anything ahead too quickly. Today there is opportunity to observe your world and your current circumstances from all angles… when processed fully the way will become clear.

New Moon Global Timings:

Los Angeles, USA	Sat, 17 Jun 2023 at 21:36 PDT
New York, USA	Sun, 18 Jun 2023 at 00:36 EDT
Reykjavik, Iceland	Sun, 18 Jun 2023 at 04:36 GMT
London, United Kingdom	Sun, 18 Jun 2023 at 05:36 BST
Paris, France	Sun, 18 Jun 2023 at 06:36 CEST
Cape Town, South Africa	Sun, 18 Jun 2023 at 06:36 SAST
Delhi, India	Sun, 18 Jun 2023 at 10:06 IST
Perth, Australia	Sun, 18 Jun 2023 at 12:36 AWST
Tokyo, Japan	Sun, 18 Jun 2023 at 13:36 JST
Sydney, Australia	Sun, 18 Jun 2023 at 14:36 AEST
Auckland, New Zealand	Sun, 18 Jun 2023 at 16:36 NZST
Greenwich Mean Time, GMT	Sun, 18 Jun 2023 at 04:36 GMT

The Waxing Crescent Moon – from June 19th – 25th passing through Cancer, Leo, Virgo and into Libra.

The essence of this Moon phase is about putting wrongs to right and letting go of old structures and systems that no longer serve and doing the stuff we need to do to make this possible, with Saturn shifting into retrograde to honor this process.

Inevitably during periods of accelerated change, we experience resistance, both inside or out, and at the time of the Solstice on the 21st, we see the potential for some quite highly charged reactive behaviors... but the Solstice in itself is a time of natural transition, and so as far as positive change is concerned, the Universe seriously has your back, so lean into this shift and use the energy to support your own growth and evolution.

The First Quarter Moon – June 26th Libra.

The Lunar flow of this first quarter Moon actually feels rather busy and fairly fast paced... but also potentially very productive!

The pull of energy is seeking balance and harmony, so whatever shifts were happening in your world over the Solstice period, take stock today taking into account the way that your heart is feeling, balanced with the objectivity of your mind... and then it's full steam ahead!

The Waxing Gibbous Moon – from June 27th into July passing through Libra into Scorpio.

The forward motion of this Moon phase feels steady and set to plough ahead whether internally or in your external manifestations. So, consolidate, invest, and grow!

The Lunar energy on the 30th taps into the very changeable influence of Uranus, plus Neptune begins a retrograde period which can sometimes initiate some emotional fog, so if any disruptions occur, trust that you need to see something more clearly and if necessary, tweak and course correct before continuing on your way.

29 Monday
Virgo / VOC / Libra

Memorial Day USA
UK Spring Bank Holiday

30 Tuesday
Libra

31 Wednesday
Libra / VOC / Scorpio

1 Thursday
Scorpio

2 Friday
Scorpio

Waxing Gibbous Moon Phase Ends

Journaling and Notes

3 Saturday
Scorpio / VOC / Sagittarius

Full Moon 13°17' Sagittarius

4 Sunday
Sagittarius

Full Moon 13°17' Sagittarius

5 Monday
Sagittarius / VOC / Capricorn

Waning Gibbous Moon Phase Begins

6 Tuesday
Capricorn

7 Wednesday
Capricorn / VOC / Aquarius

8 Thursday
Aquarius

9 Friday
Aquarius / VOC / Pisces

Waning Gibbous Moon Phase Ends

Journaling and Notes

10 Saturday

Pisces

Last Quarter Moon Pisces

11 Sunday

Pisces / VOC / Aries

Waning Crescent Moon Phase Begins

12 Monday
Aries

13 Tuesday
Aries / VOC / Taurus

14 Wednesday
Taurus

15 Thursday
Taurus

16 Friday
Taurus / VOC / Gemini

Journaling and Notes

---

17 **Saturday**

Gemini

New Moon 26°42' Gemini
Saturn Retrograde Begins

---

18 **Sunday**

Gemini / VOC / Cancer

New Moon 26°42' Gemini
UK, USA & Canada Father's Day

---

19 Monday
Cancer

Waxing Crescent Moon Phase Begins

20 Tuesday
Cancer / VOC / Leo

21 Wednesday
Leo

Summer Solstice Northern Hemisphere – Winter Solstice Southern Hemisphere
Sun Enters Cancer

22 Thursday
Leo / VOC

23 Friday
VOC / Virgo

Journaling and Notes

24 Saturday
Virgo

25 Sunday
Virgo / VOC / Libra

Waxing Crescent Moon Phase Ends

26 Monday
Libra

First Quarter Moon Libra

27 Tuesday
Libra

Waxing Gibbous Moon Phase Begins

28 Wednesday
Libra / VOC / Scorpio

29 Thursday
Scorpio

30 Friday
Scorpio / VOC / Sagittarius

Neptune Retrograde Begins

Journaling and Notes

1 Saturday
Sagittarius

2 Sunday
Sagittarius / VOC / Capricorn

Waxing Gibbous Moon Phase Ends

Desires, Goals, and Intentions for July 2023

Welcome to July 2023

July 2023. Karmic openings and walking the talk!

The overall astro-dynamics of July create an environment that is calling for change with a ton of opportunities to understand that what we do in the here and now is creating the future.

In principle I am sure that we all know this, however, this month looks to bring this into our awareness in real terms, and with purpose. There is a strong flavor of Karmic happenings that call us as individuals and as a collective humanity, to walk our talk!

The Full Moon in Capricorn on the 3rd is primed for expansion whilst also holding the potential to illuminate new ways of addressing old problems from a balanced perspective, and the New Moon in Cancer on the 17th and 18th supports healing through balance and gentle nurture. With balanced Venus, and Chiron the wounded healer, both moving into retrograde on the 23rd I think this will be a truly interesting month.

And whilst the overall energy is pushing forwards continually, the Lunar influence supports pockets of time for you to reflect, find clarity of purpose, and engage in those important communications and conversations that move your manifestations forwards, and in real terms.

In this powerful month we are guided by the Cards of Independence and Restore Balance, supported by Teiwaz, the Rune of the Spiritual Warrior and Ehwaz, the Rune of Movement, highlighting the incredible potential held within our collective humanity.

Teiwaz, the Rune of the Spiritual Warrior speaks of discernment and the need to recognize what constitutes health within our relationships. This theme is reinforced by the card of Independence that calls you to establish a healthy inter-dependency within all your relationships that honors and respects the needs of all parties.

Additional messages and guidance.

Both individually and/or as a collective humanity, this card and Rune are asking questions. Do you and/or we as a collective give more than we take… or is it the other way around… taking more than we give?

In a dynamic month of powerful potential opportunity for evaluation and action, this card calls us as a collective humanity to recognize our inter-dependency not only with each other as human beings, but with all of life, and in particular, our relationship with our planet without whom we cannot exist.

Cards and Runes July 2023

The combination of Ehwaz, the Rune of Movement and the card of Restore Balance, suggests momentum with the potential to better any situation through restoring and maintaining balance and harmony.

Additional messages and guidance.

Consciously developing our awareness is one of the greatest gifts that we can offer ourselves. Life is a continual stream of experience, and when we are able to notice both the circumstances that resonate with us, supporting our internal balance and harmony, and also situations that do the opposite, discombobulating our energy and leaving us feeling fragmented or uncertain, this level of awareness enables us to navigate our lives from a position of mindful empowerment.

You are called to develop the skill of consciously noticing yourself, and actively using your new levels of awareness to enhance your ability to navigate life from a position of mindfulness, creating ongoing centeredness and balance within yourself in any situation.

Moon Phases July 2023

The Waxing Gibbous Moon – from June 27th - July 2nd passing through Libra, Scorpio and into Sagittarius.

The forward motion of this Moon phase feels steady and set to plough ahead whether internally or in your external manifestations. So, consolidate, invest, and grow!

The Lunar energy on the 30th taps into the very changeable influence of Uranus, so if any disruptions occur, trust that you need to see something more clearly and if necessary, tweak and course correct before continuing on your way. You may well feel the emotional impact of these interruptions/distractions on the 1st July but this will be fleeting. The overall build up to the Full Moon is remarkably reflective and positive!

The Full Moon – July 3rd - 11° 18' Capricorn.

Whilst this Full Moon in earthy ambitious Capricorn is primed for expansion, the Lunar influence may also highlight any insecurities about achieving success, believing in yourself, and taking an ownership of your greatest potential. However, there is also the potential that this Moon will illuminate new ways of addressing old problems from a balanced perspective.
Given the underlying shifts and turns of the last few weeks, this looks to be an interesting Moon of significant potential.

Full Moon Global Timings:

Los Angeles, USA	Mon, 3 Jul 2023 at 04:38 PDT
New York, USA	Mon, 3 Jul 2023 at 07:38 EDT
Reykjavik, Iceland	Mon, 3 Jul 2023 at 11:38 GMT
London, United Kingdom	Mon, 3 Jul 2023 at 12:38 BST
Paris, France	Mon, 3 Jul 2023 at 13:38 CEST
Cape Town, South Africa	Mon, 3 Jul 2023 at 13:38 SAST
Delhi, India	Mon, 3 Jul 2023 at 17:08 IST
Perth, Australia	Mon, 3 Jul 2023 at 19:38 AWST
Tokyo, Japan	Mon, 3 Jul 2023 at 20:38 JST
Sydney, Australia	Mon, 3 Jul 2023 at 21:38 AEST
Auckland, New Zealand	Mon, 3 Jul 2023 at 23:38 NZST
Greenwich Mean Time, GMT	Mon, 3 Jul 2023 at 11:38 GMT

The Disseminating or Waning Gibbous Moon – from July 4th – 9th passing through Capricorn, Aquarius, Pisces, and into Aries.

Despite the steadying influence of the disseminating Moon the Lunar influence of this phase is remarkably strong with some significant surges of rather impulsive energy, particularly on the 4th, 6th, and 8th, so there's quite an ebb and flow kind of momentum happening, always moving ahead but with surges that come with an additional push!

However, all of this comes with a higher purpose. The current overall astro-dynamics are highlighting the connection between past actions and present circumstances with a massive push to change the way that we do things and to fix and heal so we can create a different future.

Whatever was illuminated at the Full Moon, use this phase to observe, notice, and process thoroughly.

The Last Quarter Moon July 10th – Aries.

The Lunar influence today suggests a welcome moment of pause that invites you to embrace the ethos of healing and reparation.

So, press the pause button...
Acknowledge and accept the things that you can't change...
Recognize what you can change in the present time...

And commit fully to take active steps that initiate healing and the creation of a different future.

The Balsamic Moon or Waning Crescent Moon – from July 11th – 16th passing through Taurus, Gemini, and into Cancer.

It's time to talk... with others... and with ourselves! This Moon phase begins with a powerful dynamic that asks you to step up and walk your talk.

The overall flow of Lunar influence at this time may not feel particularly gentle but the opportunities to see things from all perspectives and gain understanding really do feel immense.

In your personal manifestations you can seek clarity in any areas of our lives that have been feeling uncertain or blocked.

The New Moon – July 17th / 18th - 24° 55' Cancer.

This New Moon is loaded with Karmic potential with energy that is absolutely primed to move your wishes and intentions forwards... and fast!

A Cancer Moon will naturally invite you to focus on your sense of belonging, your home, and your family and the overall dynamics today will strongly support any wishes and intentions that bring balance to these areas of your life. Given the overall flavor of the astro-dynamics that are emphasizing shifts and change, if you are someone who struggles with anxiety at times of transition this is an ideal New Moon to set wishes and intentions to bring you emotional strength, stability, resilience, and peace of mind.

New Moon Global Timings:

Los Angeles, USA	Mon, 17 Jul 2023 at 11:31 PDT
New York, USA	Mon, 17 Jul 2023 at 14:31 EDT
Reykjavik, Iceland	Mon, 17 Jul 2023 at 18:31 GMT
London, United Kingdom	Mon, 17 Jul 2023 at 19:31 BST
Paris, France	Mon, 17 Jul 2023 at 20:31 CEST
Cape Town, South Africa	Mon, 17 Jul 2023 at 20:31 SAST
Delhi, India	Tue, 18 Jul 2023 at 00:01 IST
Perth, Australia	Tue, 18 Jul 2023 at 02:31 AWST
Tokyo, Japan	Tue, 18 Jul 2023 at 03:31 JST
Sydney, Australia	Tue, 18 Jul 2023 at 04:31 AEST
Auckland, New Zealand	Tue, 18 Jul 2023 at 06:31 NZST
Greenwich Mean Time, GMT	Mon, 17 Jul 2023 at 18:31 GMT

The Waxing Crescent Moon – from July 19th – 24th passing through Leo, Virgo and into Libra.

The pace and ups and downs of the Lunar influence during this Moon phase feels fast and changeable and with both lovely balanced Venus and Chiron the wounded healer both moving into retrograde on the 23rd if you find yourself feeling uncertain, or as if you just get started, you know where you're going, and then suddenly you find yourself changing direction, or moving from one thing to another... well you are well in tune with the Lunar happenings!

So take it easy and cut yourself some slack...

Try to be an observer as well as a participant... sometimes slowing down can be just as productive as trying to plough ahead all of the time and at full speed!

The First Quarter Moon – July 25th / 26th – Libra / Scorpio.

The dynamics of this first quarter Moon span the time when the Moon passes from Libra into Scorpio between the 25th and 26th and the Lunar energy taps straight into the Karmic energetic that is calling for re-birth and transformation.

The Quarter Moons are always associated with review and the opportunity to see exactly what you need to do to move ahead, whether this is continuing as you are and staying on track or seeing what you need to course correct and re-establish a new direction. Either way, this Moon has a real flavor of destiny about it, so listen up and respond to whatever life brings.

The Waxing Gibbous Moon – from July 27th – 31st passing through Scorpio, Sagittarius, and Capricorn.

This Moon phase begins by inviting you to see beyond the obvious. The Lunar energy then brings a continual flow of motivated and happening energy that backs you 100% to take real pragmatic and practical actions to move your manifestations forwards. Be sure to ground yourself from time to time as the energy during this Moon phase is on the move!

3 Monday
Capricorn

Full Moon 11°18' Capricorn

4 Tuesday
Capricorn / VOC / Aquarius

Waning Gibbous Moon Phase Begins
USA Independence Day

5 Wednesday
Aquarius

6 Thursday
Aquarius / VOC /Pisces

7 Friday
Pisces

Journaling and Notes

8 **Saturday**

Pisces / VOC / Aries

9 **Sunday**

Aries

Waning Gibbous Moon Phase Ends

10 Monday
Aries / VOC / Taurus

Last Quarter Moon Aries

11 Tuesday
Taurus

Waning Crescent Moon Phase Begins

12 Wednesday
Taurus

13 Thursday
Taurus / VOC / Gemini

14 Friday
Gemini

Journaling and Notes

15 Saturday
Gemini / VOC / Cancer

16 Sunday
Cancer

Waning Crescent Moon Phase Ends

17 Monday
Cancer

New Moon 24°55' Cancer

18 Tuesday
Cancer / VOC / Leo

New Moon 24°55' Cancer

19 Wednesday
Leo

Waxing Crescent Moon Phase Begins

20 Thursday
Leo / VOC / Virgo

21 Friday
Virgo

Journaling and Notes

22 **Saturday**
Virgo

Sun Enters Leo

23 **Sunday**
Virgo / VOC / Libra

Sun Enters Leo
Chiron Retrograde Begins
Venus Retrograde Begins

24 Monday
Libra

Waxing Crescent Moon Phase Ends

25 Tuesday
Libra / VOC / Scorpio

First Quarter Moon Libra / Scorpio

26 Wednesday
Scorpio

First Quarter Moon Libra / Scorpio

27 Thursday
Scorpio / VOC

Waxing Gibbous Moon Phase Begins

28 Friday
VOC / Sagittarius

Journaling and Notes

29 Saturday
Sagittarius / VOC

30 Sunday
VOC / Capricorn

Desires, Goals, and Intentions for August 2023

Welcome to August 2023

August 2023. A month of illumination!

This is a month of two Super Full Moons! The second Moon is a Blue Moon.

On the 1st and 2nd the Aquarius Moon, which is also Lunar Lammas in the Northern Hemisphere and Imbolc in the Southern hemisphere, has a distinct overall flavor of 'waking up' about it, bringing opportunity for serious thinking, and the energy to then take action… and the Super Blue Moon on the 30th and 31st in deeply sensitive and spiritual Pisces could bring you exactly what you need to see to find clarification if you are uncertain about any aspects of your future plans or you are seeking guidance about your calling and your purpose. Uranus the great awakener also moves into retrograde on the 29th, supporting conscious innovative actions that forge new ways of being and living.

So although the Lunar energy this month does suggest the potential for progression, I really do feel that this is a month when prioritizing internal growth and evaluation will pay dividends. This doesn't mean that progress won't happen in your external circumstances… more that trying to plough ahead with speed could ultimately slow you down.

The New Moon on the 16th looks to bring massive windows of major opportunity especially in enhancing your leadership skills and your personal growth and confidence, including letting go of internal blocks in these areas of your world.

The overall flow of this month seems to promote progress through illumination, becoming an observer of your world and then with reflection and the digestion of all that is shown, taking responsive and appropriate actions.

This flow of energy is supported by our cards of Worth the Wait with Isa the Rune of Standstill and Don't Wobble supported by Raido the Rune of Journey, suggesting that in our goal driven society it is incredibly helpful to give yourself permission to slow down and discover the benefits that come from being truly present.

Cards and Runes August 2023

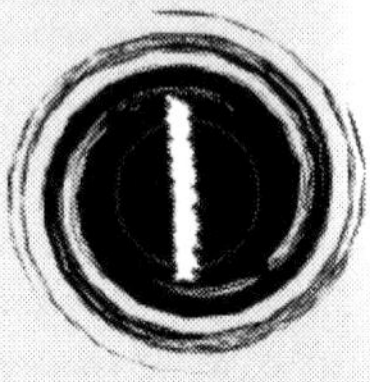

The card of Worth the Wait supported by Isa the Rune of Standstill invites you to recognize that standing still and becoming fully present can sometimes be the most effective way to progress.

Additional messages and guidance.
The message of this card is patience.

Allow your situation to unfold, far more is taking place behind the scenes then you are currently able to see.

Centre yourself in a space of gratitude and appreciation for all that you have and all that you are right now… and trust that everything is unfolding and emerging just as it should.

Cards and Runes August 2023

The card of Don't Wobble acknowledges the power and impact of change with reassurance that any feelings of anxiety or uncertainty are completely normal. Supported by Raido the Rune of Journey, an inward journey of meditation is advised, as well as assurances that progression will occur.

Additional messages and guidance.
This card brings a clear message. You are facing tough choices that are raising your levels of anxiety. Whatever your situation, this card is here to validate the decisions and the choices that you are making. You know that something has to change, and deep down you know what you need to do. It is time to take action.

Find a form of meditation that works for you. Either traditional meditation, or perhaps a walking meditation, where you connect with nature. Whatever you do, take time every day to center yourself, to get still, and to connect with the support of the universe that surrounds you.

Let go of any self-doubt and trust your inner knowing.

Moon Phases August 2023

The Super Full Moon – August 1st / 2nd - 9° 15' Aquarius.

The feel of this Moon is strong... but also loaded with potential. An Aquarius Full Moon naturally opens a space of insight and higher guidance to bring clarity and point us in the right direction and the dynamics of this particular Full Moon, which align with the Earth Festival of Lammas in the northern hemisphere and Imbolc in the southern hemisphere, has a distinct overall flavor of 'waking up' about it, bringing opportunity for serious thinking, and the energy to then take action!

So if this Moon brings anything to the surface that presses your buttons or makes you wobble, the energy is very supportive of resolution and healing through conscious awareness and mindful thought.

Full Moon Global Timings:

Los Angeles, USA	Tue, 1 Aug 2023 at 11:31 PDT
New York, USA	Tue, 1 Aug 2023 at 14:31 EDT
Reykjavik, Iceland	Tue, 1 Aug 2023 at 18:31 GMT
London, United Kingdom	Tue, 1 Aug 2023 at 19:31 BST
Paris, France	Tue, 1 Aug 2023 at 20:31 CEST
Cape Town, South Africa	Tue, 1 Aug 2023 at 20:31 SAST
Delhi, India	Wed, 2 Aug 2023 at 00:01 IST
Perth, Australia	Wed, 2 Aug 2023 at 02:31 AWST
Tokyo, Japan	Wed, 2 Aug 2023 at 03:31 JST
Sydney, Australia	Wed, 2 Aug 2023 at 04:31 AEST
Auckland, New Zealand	Wed, 2 Aug 2023 at 06:31 NZST
Greenwich Mean Time, GMT	Tue, 1 Aug 2023 at 18:31 GMT

The Disseminating or Waning Gibbous Moon – from August 3rd – 7th passing through Aquarius, Pisces, Aries, and into Taurus.

On the one hand, the energy of this Moon phase is promoting forward movement and continued momentum, and this is marvelous in any areas of our manifestations that are already in flow and on track... fabulous!

However,... if something you want to happen just isn't quite ready or is feeling a bit stuck or entrenched, the flow of forward motion could feel a bit pressured, so go easy on yourself and focus on the things that you can do rather than the things that haven't quite got going yet.

The Last Quarter Moon August 8th – Taurus.

The dynamics of this last quarter Moon are refreshingly positive bringing a Lunar infusion of creativity, hopefulness, and optimism.

Given the overall strength of the planetary happenings at the moment, all pushing for change, this lens of positivity is just delightful, really helping you to evaluate and assess through the eyes of possibility.

The Balsamic Moon or Waning Crescent Moon – from August 9th – 15th passing through Taurus, Gemini, Cancer, and into Leo.

This Moon phase gets off to a slightly intense start so whatever you feel passionate about, good, or bad, harness the energy to invest steadily rather than ploughing ahead like a bull in a china shop... because the Lunar influence then gently levels out bringing a much calmer vibe, with an opportunity to view any situation from all angles before moving ahead.

The Lunar flow gathers in intensity once more on the 14th with the potential for creative ideas/solutions to emerge on the 15th, so be particularly aware of signs and synchronicities at this time.

The New Moon – August 16th - 23° 16' Leo.

The dynamics of this New Moon looks to bring massive windows of major opportunities so if you are only going to use one New Moon this year to set wishes and intentions then I would personally recommend this one!

A Leo New Moon naturally invites wishes that enhance your personal passions and your leadership qualities, bringing enthusiasm and determination, whilst building your confidence and individual self-expression, and the astro-dynamics today invite you to address the past, heal the past, and free you to take bold steps into a new and brighter future!

New Moon Global Timings

Los Angeles, USA	Wed, 16 Aug 2023 at 02:37 PDT
New York, USA	Wed, 16 Aug 2023 at 05:37 EDT
Reykjavik, Iceland	Wed, 16 Aug 2023 at 09:37 GMT
London, United Kingdom	Wed, 16 Aug 2023 at 10:37 BST
Paris, France	Wed, 16 Aug 2023 at 11:37 CEST
Cape Town, South Africa	Wed, 16 Aug 2023 at 11:37 SAST
Delhi, India	Wed, 16 Aug 2023 at 15:07 IST

Perth, Australia	Wed, 16 Aug 2023 at 17:37 AWST
Tokyo, Japan	Wed, 16 Aug 2023 at 18:37 JST
Sydney, Australia	Wed, 16 Aug 2023 at 19:37 AEST
Auckland, New Zealand	Wed, 16 Aug 2023 at 21:37 NZST
Greenwich Mean Time, GMT	Wed, 16 Aug 2023 at 09:37 GMT

The Waxing Crescent Moon – from August 17th – 23rd passing through Virgo, Libra, and into Scorpio.

The start of this Moon phase may well bring a sense of impatience and a desire to just get going and make stuff happen… but don't be too hasty. From the 17th – 19th the Lunar influence supports meticulous and methodical working within a sensible timetable. The 20th brings a very different dynamic that could potentially slow you down, so paying attention to the details early in this phase is a really good idea.

From the 21st we see renewed energy that supports good communications with growth and movement and with Mercury moving into retrograde on the 23rd be mindful that sometimes communications can arrive in the form of unexpected delays and interruptions.

The First Quarter Moon – August 24th - Sagittarius.

The first quarter Moon always requests some sort of review, and the focus of today's Lunar input supports progress and the overcoming of any form of difficulty through holding a positive mindset and the reassessing of your goals in real terms and seeing what needs doing right here and right now. A great energetic combination that holds a space of realistic and empowered evaluation.

The Waxing Gibbous Moon – from August 25th – 29th passing through Sagittarius, Capricorn, and Aquarius.

Despite holding a very steady and consistent increase in energy, this Moon phase has a reflective feel to it with the potential for signs and synchronicities to show up particularly around the 26th and 28th, so in your manifestations and personal energy flow, observe and digest, alongside continual and measured progress.

The Super Full Moon – Blue Moon - August 30th / 31st - 7° 24’ Pisces.

A Blue moon happens when we get two Full Moon’s in the same month and traditionally they are said to boost the influence of the Zodiac sign that they are in and also to illuminate your hopes and wishes for the future.

Given that this Moon is in deeply sensitive and spiritual Pisces if you are seeking guidance about your calling and your purpose, or you are uncertain about any aspects of your future plans then the energy of this Full Moon could bring you exactly what you need to see to find clarification.

Personally, I would suggest approaching this day very consciously and using the influence to the max. If you have ever considered going on a spiritual retreat or committing to a full day of meditation then this is the day to do it!

Full Moon - Blue Moon Global Timings:

Los Angeles, USA	Wed, 30 Aug 2023 at 18:35 PDT
New York, USA	Wed, 30 Aug 2023 at 21:35 EDT
Reykjavik, Iceland	Thu, 31 Aug 2023 at 01:35 GMT
London, United Kingdom	Thu, 31 Aug 2023 at 02:35 BST
Paris, France	Thu, 31 Aug 2023 at 03:35 CEST
Cape Town, South Africa	Thu, 31 Aug 2023 at 03:35 SAST
Delhi, India	Thu, 31 Aug 2023 at 07:05 IST
Perth, Australia	Thu, 31 Aug 2023 at 09:35 AWST
Tokyo, Japan	Thu, 31 Aug 2023 at 10:35 JST
Sydney, Australia	Thu, 31 Aug 2023 at 11:35 AEST
Auckland, New Zealand	Thu, 31 Aug 2023 at 13:35 NZST
Greenwich Mean Time, GMT	Thu, 31 Aug 2023 at 01:35 GMT

31 **Monday**
Capricorn

Waxing Gibbous Moon Phase Ends

1 **Tuesday**
Capricorn / VOC / Aquarius

Lammas Northern Hemisphere - Imbolc Southern Hemisphere
Super Full Moon 9°15' Aquarius

2 **Wednesday**
Aquarius / VOC

Super Full Moon 9°15' Aquarius

3 **Thursday**
VOC / Pisces

Waning Gibbous Moon Phase Begins

4 **Friday**
Pisces

Journaling and Notes

5 Saturday
Pisces / VOC / Aries

6 Sunday
Aries

7 Monday
Aries / VOC / Taurus

Waning Gibbous Moon Phase Ends

8 Tuesday
Taurus

Last Quarter Moon Taurus

9 Wednesday
Taurus / VOC / Gemini

United Nations Indigenous People's Day
Waning Crescent Moon Phase Begins

10 Thursday
Gemini

11 Friday
Gemini / VOC / Cancer

Journaling and Notes

12 Saturday
Cancer

13 Sunday
Cancer

14 **Monday**
Cancer / VOC / Leo

15 **Tuesday**
Leo

Waning Crescent Moon Phase Ends

16 **Wednesday**
Leo / VOC / Virgo

New Moon 23°16’ Leo

17 **Thursday**
Virgo

Waxing Crescent Moon Phase Begins

18 **Friday**
Virgo

Journaling and Notes

19 Saturday

Virgo / VOC / Libra

20 Sunday

Libra

21 Monday
Libra / VOC / Scorpio

22 Tuesday
Scorpio

23 Wednesday
Scorpio

Waxing Crescent Moon Phase Ends
Mercury Retrograde Begins
Sun Enters Virgo

24 Thursday
Scorpio / VOC / Sagittarius

First Quarter Moon Sagittarius

25 Friday
Sagittarius

Waxing Gibbous Moon Phase Begins

Journaling and Notes

26 Saturday

Sagittarius / VOC / Capricorn

27 Sunday

Capricorn

28 Monday
Capricorn / VOC / Aquarius

UK Late Summer Bank Holiday

29 Tuesday
Aquarius

Waxing Gibbous Moon Phase Ends
Uranus Retrograde Begins

30 Wednesday
Aquarius / VOC / Pisces

Super Full Blue Moon 7°24’ Pisces

31 Thursday
Pisces

Super Full Blue Moon 7°24’ Pisces

1 Friday
Pisces / VOC / Aries

Waning Gibbous Moon Phase Begins

Journaling and Notes

2 Saturday

Aries

3 Sunday

Aries / VOC Taurus

Australia & New Zealand Father's Day

Desires, Goals, and Intentions for September 2023

Welcome to September 2023

September 2023. Incorporate what you've learned... it's time to implement, heal, and grow!

In terms of your personal growth and evolution and how this fuels your manifestations... we all know that change starts from within and the Lunar flow of energy during September suggests a series of opportunities that enable you to genuinely start to incorporate your learning and observations from August into real and solid potential manifestations working from the inside out.

Although Venus starts to move forwards on the 4th, Jupiter moves into retrograde on same day, and with Mercury still in retrograde until the 15th, if at any time you feel your progress is hampered or your buttons are being pressed, then trust that situations, circumstances, and relationships are being brought to your attention because adjustments are needed.

The New Moon in Virgo on the 14th and 15th is absolutely primed to sow seeds and initiate new opportunities, and also to overcome and let go of any aspects of your own internal thinking patterns or attitudes and behaviors that involve self-criticism and/or procrastination. Yea!

The dynamics of the natural turning point of the Autumn Equinox in the northern hemisphere and the Spring Equinox in the southern hemisphere on the 23rd followed by the Full Moon in Aries on the 29th are likely to illuminate all the stuff that is working and on track in your world... and also all the stuff that isn't, so listen up.

The overall dynamics of this month seems to support busyness with pockets of heightened awareness that are designed to re-establish balance and bring opportunities to find clarity and creative resolutions.

This rather buzzy and somewhat inconsistent flow of energy is supported by our Cards of Internal Dialogue with Othila, the Rune of Separation, and Ground Yourself with Raido, the Rune of Journey, inviting you appreciate the opportunities in every situation, remain grounded, and to enjoy the ride.

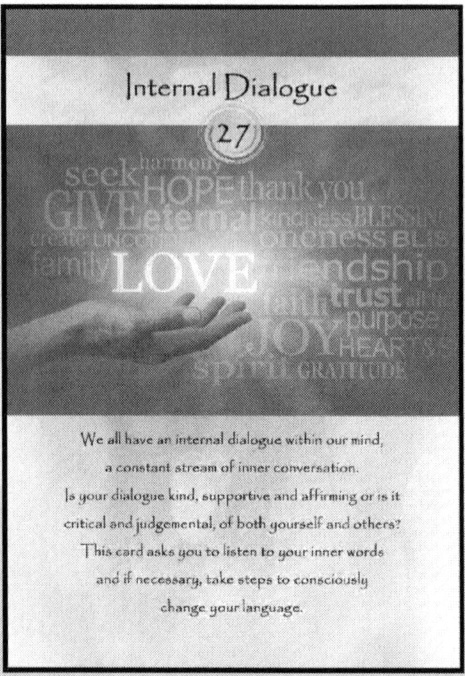

Othila, the Rune of Separation, combined with the card of Internal Dialogue asks you to recognize the nature of your thinking and let go of any inappropriate negativity.

Additional messages and guidance.
Words carry power! A charismatic leader can inspire an audience to step up and be the very best version of themselves… or… a charismatic leader can inflame an audience into committing acts of atrocity that step over any boundaries of what would constitute a decent human being.

Are the words within your mind voiced through grace, promoting love and kindness to both yourself and others, or other judgmental, critical, harsh, and cynical, causing stress and distress. Almost everyone when they first listen to their internal dialogue will discover a proportion of negativity, and also grievance, within this language. Not only does this cause damage to yourself, creating disharmony within, but the energetic resonance of these words will also attract more of the same in your external world. Listen to the language in your mind and make a firm commitment to create words of inspiration.

Cards and Runes September 2023

The card of Ground Yourself supported by Raido the Rune of Journey, showing up a second month in a row, reminds you that journeying into nature and connecting with the Earth will help to keep you grounded even when the pace of life is hectic buzzy and inconsistent.

Additional messages and guidance.
Are you struggling to feel grounded or centered? Has a life event thrown you a curve ball, leaving you feeling as though there is no solid ground beneath you? At any given time during the course of our lives, events can take place that leave us feeling vulnerable, wobbly, and out of balance. This card asks you to literally ground yourself.

Find somewhere where you can reconnect with nature, even in a city there are always places where you can go. If you are unable to get your bare feet onto the ground, then find a tree in the street and ask it if you may sit with it for a while. You will hear the answer clearly. Or perhaps literally put your hands into some soil. One way or the other you are asked to plug yourself into the energy of the Earth.

Moon Phases September 2023

The Disseminating or Waning Gibbous Moon – from September 1st – 5th passing through Pisces, Aries, Taurus, and into Gemini.

This Moon phase brings a distinct series of steps in energy flow.

On the 1st the illuminations of the Blue Moon are beautifully continued emphasizing your spiritual purpose, pathway, and calling.

This then flows into the energetics on the 2nd that urge you to transform and birth these ideals into reality… but go steady and don't be too hasty or impulsive… because the energy on the 3rd may well bring signs, signals, and synchronicities to guide and inform.

On the 4th the Lunar input invites you to get into a steady productive flow… and if any interruptions occur on the 5th then take note, this is most likely to be useful information to assist your evaluations at the Last Quarter.

The Last Quarter Moon - September 6th / 7th – Gemini.

In manifestation, this Last Quarter Moon supports clarity of intent through awareness of your part and your connection to the bigger picture and there is ample opportunity in the overall astro-dynamics today to show you exactly what you need to see/hear/do to continue to expand and progress.

The Balsamic Moon or Waning Crescent Moon – from September 8th – 13th passing through Cancer, Leo, and into Virgo.

Despite the diminishing of the Lunar energy this Moon phase begins with a strong sense of gentle, nurturing, perseverance.

The 10th may feel a little more dynamic and intense with a surge of energy that could disrupt or push forwards… or both!

The Lunar influence on the 12th will remind you of what really matters and speak to you from the heart, so take any yearnings seriously and be particularly gentle with yourself on the 13th… any underlying pressures you feel today will soon pass with renewed energy and vigor returning.

The New Moon – September 14th / 15th - 21° 58’ Virgo.

The overall astro-dynamics that support this New Moon are absolutely primed to not simply sow seeds and initiate new opportunities, but also to overcome and let go of any aspects of your own internal thinking patterns or attitudes and behaviors that involve self-criticism and/or procrastination.

The Lunar connections of this particular New Moon in Virgo invites you to expand your perspectives, overcome personal insecurities, and discover and implement higher minded solutions that consider a sustainable future, with new ways of seeing, being, and doing, not just for you, but for future generations yet to come.

New Moon Global Timings:

Los Angeles, USA	Thu, 14 Sep 2023 at 18:39 PDT
New York, USA	Thu, 14 Sep 2023 at 21:39 EDT
Reykjavik, Iceland	Fri, 15 Sep 2023 at 01:39 GMT
London, United Kingdom	Fri, 15 Sep 2023 at 02:39 BST
Paris, France	Fri, 15 Sep 2023 at 03:39 CEST
Cape Town, South Africa	Fri, 15 Sep 2023 at 03:39 SAST
Delhi, India	Fri, 15 Sep 2023 at 07:09 IST
Perth, Australia	Fri, 15 Sep 2023 at 09:39 AWST
Tokyo, Japan	Fri, 15 Sep 2023 at 10:39 JST
Sydney, Australia	Fri, 15 Sep 2023 at 11:39 AEST
Auckland, New Zealand	Fri, 15 Sep 2023 at 13:39 NZST
Greenwich Mean Time, GMT	Fri, 15 Sep 2023 at 01:39 GMT

The Waxing Crescent Moon – from September 16th – 21st passing through Libra, Scorpio, and into Sagittarius.

The start of this Moon phase begins with a super flow of harmony and balance... however, the Lunar influence grows in intensity on the 17th so if buttons are pressed, then listen up... it’s time to heal and rebalance.

The Lunar input supports constructive progress on the 18th followed by some interesting and changeable energy over the 19th and 20th, so take life as it comes and be responsive in the moment. As we head towards the First Quarter energetics of review the pressure eases.

The First Quarter Moon – September 22nd - Sagittarius.

Creativity definitely rules the day today! The First Quarter Moon always invites evaluation and review, and the overall astro-dynamics suggest that you might feel and underlying sense of urgency or even impatience… so use the energy and channel it well… the Lunar connections have a strong flavor of creativity and imaginative potential.

The Waxing Gibbous Moon – from September 23rd – 28th passing through Capricorn, Aquarius, and Pisces.

The overall flow of this Lunar phase feels quite buzzy and active, with a heightened awareness of where you've come from, and where you may wish to be heading…

However, the momentum of the growing Moon may not always flow with a consistent pace, so… in attitude, keep a good head on your shoulders… and in your actions… hold your course and persevere.

The Full Moon – September 29th - 6° 00' Aries.

A Full Moon in Aries is set to inspire you to pursue your dreams with passion, illuminating the areas of your world that are on track and deserve further investment … and also those areas of your life that are not working so well and therefore need an investment of a different kind!

The overall astro-dynamics of the day suggest an emphasis on relationships and communication. So, celebrate the people you love and the dynamics of the joyous and balanced relationships of your world… and if any aspect of imbalance within relationships shows up, take it seriously and take time to contemplate how best to move these situations forwards in ways that honor and respect all parties.

Full Moon Global Timings:

Los Angeles, USA	Fri, 29 Sep 2023 at 02:57 PDT
New York, USA	Fri, 29 Sep 2023 at 05:57 EDT
Reykjavik, Iceland	Fri, 29 Sep 2023 at 09:57 GMT
London, United Kingdom	Fri, 29 Sep 2023 at 10:57 BST
Paris, France	Fri, 29 Sep 2023 at 11:57 CEST
Cape Town, South Africa	Fri, 29 Sep 2023 at 11:57 SAST
Delhi, India	Fri, 29 Sep 2023 at 15:27 IST
Perth, Australia	Fri, 29 Sep 2023 at 17:57 AWST

Tokyo, Japan	Fri, 29 Sep 2023 at 18:57 JST
Sydney, Australia	Fri, 29 Sep 2023 at 19:57 AEST
Auckland, New Zealand	Fri, 29 Sep 2023 at 22:57 NZDT
Greenwich Mean Time, GMT	Fri, 29 Sep 2023 at 09:57 GMT

The Disseminating or Waning Gibbous Moon – from September 30th into October passing through Aries.

This Waning Gibbous Moon gets off to a dynamic and fiery start, and as we move into October, even though the input of our beautiful Moon is diminishing in speed, this phase is powerful, expansive, and karmic!

4 Monday
Taurus

Labor Day – USA
Venus Retrograde Ends
Jupiter Retrograde Begins

5 Tuesday
Taurus / VOC / Gemini

Waning Gibbous Moon Phase Ends

6 Wednesday
Gemini

Last Quarter Moon Gemini

7 Thursday
Gemini / VOC

Last Quarter Moon Gemini

8 Friday
VOC / Cancer

Waning Crescent Moon Phase Begins

Journaling and Notes

9 Saturday
Cancer

10 Sunday
Cancer / VOC / Leo

11 Monday

Leo

12 Tuesday

Leo / VOC

13 Wednesday

VOC / Virgo

Waning Crescent Moon Phase Ends

14 Thursday

Virgo

New Moon 21°58’ Virgo

15 Friday

Virgo / VOC / Libra

New Moon 21°58’ Virgo
Mercury Retrograde Ends

Journaling and Notes

16 Saturday

Libra

Waxing Crescent Moon Phase Begins

17 Sunday

Libra

18 Monday
Libra / VOC / Scorpio

19 Tuesday
Scorpio

20 Wednesday
Scorpio / VOC / Sagittarius

21 Thursday
Sagittarius

Waxing Crescent Moon Phase Ends

22 Friday
Sagittarius / VOC / Capricorn

First Quarter Moon Sagittarius

Journaling and Notes

---

23 Saturday

Capricorn

Waxing Gibbous Moon Phase Begins
Autumn Equinox Northern Hemisphere – Spring Equinox Southern Hemisphere
Sun Enters Libra

---

24 Sunday

Capricorn / VOC / Aquarius

---

25 **Monday**
Aquarius

26 **Tuesday**
Aquarius / VOC

27 **Wednesday**
VOC / Pisces

28 **Thursday**
Pisces / VOC

Waxing Gibbous Moon Phase Ends

29 **Friday**
VOC / Aries

Full Moon 6°00' Aries

Journaling and Notes

30 Saturday
Aries / VOC

Waning Gibbous Moon Phase Begins

1 Sunday
VOC / Taurus

Desires, Goals, and Intentions for October 2023

Welcome to October 2023

October 2023. Cause and effect! Karmic happenings!

Eclipse season is known to herald periods of accelerated growth and change presenting windows of opportunity to address Karmic and historic wounds of the past and re-align and re-balance yourself in the present and through conscious awareness take empowered steps to create a new and different future... and the Lunar and astro-dynamics of October look to bring us opportunities to do exactly this.

For anyone to fix a problem they must first see it with clarity and then to really get the backing of the universe, approach the situation from the highest possible perspective to arrive at the most valuable, fair, productive, and peaceful, ways forward.

This is a powerful month that could well bring exactly the kinds of shifts in awareness and consciousness that assist all of humanity, both individually and as a global collective.

Just ahead of the New Moon Eclipse in Libra on the 14th and 15th, Pluto stations direct and starts to move forward. The Full Moon Eclipse in Taurus then brings an energetic of perseverance to inspire you to push ahead.

This combination of planetary events invites transformation in both your internal awareness as well as your external manifestations, and on the 31st the Earth festivals of Samhain in the northern hemisphere and Beltane in the southern hemisphere both indicate a point of new beginnings, so this really does look to be a month of movement and progression.

The guidance from our cards of Giving and Receiving and Take a Risk, combined with Kano the Rune of Openings, and Berkana the Rune of Growth, honor the potential shifts and new beginnings that are associated with Eclipse season.

Cards and Runes October 2023

The card of Giving and Receiving invites you to invest respect in all that you do and all that you plan to manifest which aligning with Kano, the Rune of Openings highlights the relationship between our internal thoughts and our external manifestations.

Additional messages and guidance.
This card asks you to re-evaluate your perspectives of 'Give and Take' within relationships.

Are you in a relationship where give and take seems to be out of balance? Are you facing circumstances in which you feel you are giving more than you are receiving and in which your contribution is either undervalued or indeed sometimes not really acknowledged at all?

Take time to reflect on the balance of giving and receiving in all of your relationships and if necessary, make adjustments, including reaching out and discussing this different perspective with all other parties involved.

Cards and Runes October 2023

The Card of Take a Risk asks you to step out of your comfort zone and collaborating with Berkana, the Rune of Growth aligns beautifully with the Eclipse energy of new beginnings and windows of opportunity.

Additional messages and guidance.
Is fear or anxiety holding you back?

There are times in life when it is appropriate to retreat and to create a safe zone for ourselves. But there is a difference between retreating to reflect, meditate and re-establish our energy, versus retreating in fear, not allowing ourselves to ever risk trying anything new.

This card brings a clear message. It is time to step out of your comfort zone and take a risk.

Moon Phases October 2023

The Disseminating or Waning Gibbous Moon – from September 30th - October 5th passing through Aries, Taurus, Gemini, and into Cancer.

This Waning Gibbous Moon gets off to a dynamic and fiery start, and as we move into October, even though the input of our beautiful Moon is diminishing in speed, this phase is powerful, expansive, and karmic... so hold onto your hats and enjoy the ride!

We enter October with an incredibly potent day leading into some hugely practical grounded productive activity that builds in potential, this is definitely a time to be stepping up... not down!

The Lunar flow of this period always honors steady consistency, so pace yourself and use the dynamic flow at its best. When the Moon moves into Gemini remember that attitude and perspective changes your personal energetic vibration, so enjoy the journey and don't be afraid to sing your own song.

The Last Quarter Moon - October 6th – Cancer.

This Last Quarter Moon is absolutely loaded with the flavor of karmic outcomes, fate, and destiny, with the potential for you to see exactly what you need to see, when you need to see it, why you need to see it... and most importantly... what steps to take next!

Given that we are approaching Eclipse season this is an important day to listen... to yourself... to others... and to the larger world around you.

The Balsamic Moon or Waning Crescent Moon – from October 7th – 13th passing through Cancer, Leo, Virgo, and into Libra.

Following such a dynamic last quarter Moon, the overall astro-energy during this phase continues in intensity holding the flavor of karmic cause and effect. On the 9th our beautiful Moon helps to ease this intensity so if your schedule allows, take a breather, and validate just how far you've come on your own personal journey of growth and evolution. As this Moon phase continues the steadying influence of the balsamic flow of energy will help you to walk your talk and prepare you for the coming Eclipse season and the opportunities that a New Moon Eclipse presents.

The New Moon Eclipse – October 14th / 15th - 21° 07' Libra.

Eclipse season is said to create a kind of energetic portal that allows us to see the relationship between past, present, and future.

Knowledge is power and the point of power is always in the Now! The decisions that we make today are creating our tomorrow... and way beyond... and a New Moon in Libra, calls for love, balance, joy, fairness, and harmony. This is a seriously amazing window of opportunity to set New Moon wishes and intentions that bring you long term happiness... and providing that it is not at the expense of the wellbeing of anyone or anything else, to receive exactly the support and guidance that you need to bring this into being, and the overall planetary connections are backing this 100%

New Moon Global Timings:

Los Angeles, USA	Sat, 14 Oct 2023 at 10:54 PDT
New York, USA	Sat, 14 Oct 2023 at 13:54 EDT
Reykjavik, Iceland	Sat, 14 Oct 2023 at 17:54 GMT
London, United Kingdom	Sat, 14 Oct 2023 at 18:54 BST
Paris, France	Sat, 14 Oct 2023 at 19:54 CEST
Cape Town, South Africa	Sat, 14 Oct 2023 at 19:54 SAST
Delhi, India	Sat, 14 Oct 2023 at 23:24 IST
Perth, Australia	Sun, 15 Oct 2023 at 01:54 AWST
Tokyo, Japan	Sun, 15 Oct 2023 at 02:54 JST
Sydney, Australia	Sun, 15 Oct 2023 at 04:54 AEDT
Auckland, New Zealand	Sun, 15 Oct 2023 at 06:54 NZDT
Greenwich Mean Time, GMT	Sat, 14 Oct 2023 at 17:54 GMT

The Waxing Crescent Moon – from October 16th – 21st passing through Scorpio, Sagittarius, and into Capricorn.

Overall, this Moon phase is fast paced and ambitious! On the 16th and 17th, the Lunar influence adds to some potentially very potent dynamics which if channeled well could kick start your manifestations into solid constructive actions.

Combine this increasing acceleration with consistent positive thinking and even if challenges present themselves, the forward motion of Lunar energy will support you in moving ahead and maintaining your flow.

The First Quarter Moon – October 22nd - Aquarius.

Stop!!! And review!!!

Today as our Moon reaches her first Quarter position we see a very long Void of Course period as the Moon passes from Capricorn into Aquarius when for 12 hours she is in neither sign. This can feel liberating or leave you feeling a bit unanchored.

Given that the Lunar influence today brings massive potential for re-birth and transformation make a conscious choice to stop and become very present to all that is going on. The information you see today will help you to know where and when to slow down, and where and when to push ahead.

The Waxing Gibbous Moon – from October 23rd – 27th passing through Aquarius, Pisces, and Aries.

The overall flow of this Lunar phase looks to gather significant momentum, with an underlying theme that asks you to expand your horizons from the inside out. Change your perspectives… change your life!

To use this energetic flow at its best, be open and available to embrace your fullest potential for creativity infused with emotional awareness and rooted in a balanced exchange of both giving and receiving.

The Full Moon Eclipse – October 28th / 29th - 5° 08' Taurus.

The energy of a Full Moon in Taurus brings perseverance and inspires you to push forwards, regardless of any obstacles in your path.

In actions of higher ideals, the energy flow will work for you, bringing staying power and stamina, however, be mindful not to act like a bull in a china shop pushing through without thought or regard… a Taurus Full Moon will also highlight areas where you might need to slow down and tread a little more lightly.

The dynamics of this Full Moon Eclipse invite you to dig deep and embrace the fullest possible learning from all your life experiences and emerge stronger and wiser with the clarity and perseverance to overcome any former insecurities that have previously held you back.

Full Moon Global Timings:

Los Angeles, USA	Sat, 28 Oct 2023 at 13:23 PDT
New York, USA	Sat, 28 Oct 2023 at 16:23 EDT
Reykjavik, Iceland	Sat, 28 Oct 2023 at 20:23 GMT
London, United Kingdom	Sat, 28 Oct 2023 at 21:23 BST
Paris, France	Sat, 28 Oct 2023 at 22:23 CEST
Cape Town, South Africa	Sat, 28 Oct 2023 at 22:23 SAST
Delhi, India	Sun, 29 Oct 2023 at 01:53 IST
Perth, Australia	Sun, 29 Oct 2023 at 04:23 AWST
Tokyo, Japan	Sun, 29 Oct 2023 at 05:23 JST
Sydney, Australia	Sun, 29 Oct 2023 at 07:23 AEDT
Auckland, New Zealand	Sun, 29 Oct 2023 at 09:23 NZDT
Greenwich Mean Time, GMT	Sat, 28 Oct 2023 at 20:23 GMT

The Disseminating or Waning Gibbous Moon – from October 30th into November passing through Taurus and Gemini.

This Moon phase sets off with a reasonably calm pace, which alongside the Earth festivals of Samhain in the northern hemisphere and Beltane in the southern hemisphere on the 31st, both indicating a point of new beginnings, invites you to mindfully integrate and consolidate your learning from Eclipse season.

The essence of achievement through mindfulness and balance continues into November.

2 Monday
Taurus

3 Tuesday
Taurus / VOC / Gemini

4 Wednesday
Gemini

5 Thursday
Gemini / VOC / Cancer

Waning Gibbous Moon Phase Ends

6 Friday
Cancer

Last Quarter Moon Cancer

Journaling and Notes

7 Saturday

Cancer / VOC / Leo

Waning Crescent Moon Phase Begins

8 Sunday

Leo

9 **Monday**
Leo

Indigenous Peoples Day - USA

10 **Tuesday**
Leo / VOC / Virgo

11 **Wednesday**
Virgo

Pluto Retrograde Ends

12 **Thursday**
Virgo / VOC

13 **Friday**
VOC / Libra

Waning Crescent Moon Phase Ends

Journaling and Notes

14 Saturday

Libra

New Moon Eclipse 21°07’ Libra

15 Sunday

Libra / VOC / Scorpio

New Moon Eclipse 21°07’ Libra

16 Monday
Scorpio

Waxing Crescent Moon Phase Begins

17 Tuesday
Scorpio / VOC / Sagittarius

18 Wednesday
Sagittarius

19 Thursday
Sagittarius / VOC

20 Friday
VOC / Capricorn

Journaling and Notes

21 **Saturday**
Capricorn

Waxing Crescent Moon Phase Ends

22 **Sunday**
Capricorn / VOC / Aquarius

First Quarter Moon Aquarius

23 Monday
Aquarius / VOC

Waxing Gibbous Moon Phase Begins
Sun Enters Scorpio

24 Tuesday
VOC / Pisces

25 Wednesday
Pisces

26 Thursday
Pisces / VOC / Aries

27 Friday
Aries

Waxing Gibbous Moon Phase Ends

Journaling and Notes

28 Saturday
Aries / VOC / Taurus

Full Moon Eclipse 5°08' Taurus

29 Sunday
Taurus

Full Moon Eclipse 5°08' Taurus
UK Clocks Change

Desires, Goals, and Intentions for November 2023

Welcome to November 2023

November 2023. Full steam ahead... inside and out... or rather outside first... then in!

Overall, November feels quite fast paced, so if at any time you feel like you need to get off the roundabout then give yourself permission to do so. We all need to catch our breath sometimes! This feels like a month when we get to connect with the stuff that really matters to us with massive opportunities to see if and how we are really stepping up and fulfilling our own personal best!

So, in areas of your world that are flying, you may suddenly find yourself flying at altitudes that were way beyond any of your former expectations... but in areas of your world that for whatever reason have taken a back seat or been put to one side, you find yourself being called to take real solid actions to bring things into balance, not just in the now, but in ways that promote longer term sustainability.

Even though several of the larger planets are still in retrograde, Saturn will station direct on the 4th, adding weight to the overall flavor of forward momentum through the month.

The dynamics of the New Moon in Scorpio on the 13th focuses on empowerment through self-mastery, whilst the Full Moon in Gemini on the 27th has quite an essence of testing around it so this will be an interesting time in of observation and evaluation in your ongoing manifestations.

Our cards this month of Course Correct and Persevere, plus Ehwaz the Rune of Movement and Fehu the Rune of Possessions validate this flow of energy and give you the heads up on how to navigate these collaborations and the overall flow of energy.

Cards and Runes November 2023

Our first card of Course Correct combined with Ehwaz the Rune of Movement which suggests the bettering of any situation, validate the fast pace of energy this month whilst reminding you to give yourself permission to pause and evaluate along the way, whilst maintaining steady progress.

Additional messages and guidance.
In our goal driven culture, we so often interpret disruptions, delays, and diversions as a negative experience, creating frustration and leaving us feeling angry or helpless.

However, if we change our perspective and trust that the universe is bringing us exactly what we need… exactly when we need it… then we can understand that even a delay or diversion is in fact a gift, bringing us a sign or a communication that we need to make some adjustments, course correct, or even take a completely different direction.

This card is here to reassure you that any delays taking place in your current situation are timely and are simply signposts to assist you in taking the next step in the right direction.

Cards and Runes November 2023

The second card this month of Persevere alongside Fehu the Rune of Possessions speaks of fulfilment and ambitions satisfied through hard work and consistent perseverance... so whatever stage of manifestation you are at... keep going!

Additional messages and guidance.
This card is an indication that you have sown seeds that contain powerful long-term possibilities. Whatever it is that you are manifesting and generating within your world, you are asked to persevere, to trust and to believe.

This card honors your diligence and the time and the effort and the hard work that you have been investing and comes to reassure you that the foundation stones you have been laying for a long-term future will come to fruition, even though further work and perseverance are required.

Have patience and continue on your pathway, one step at a time.

Moon Phases November 2023

The Disseminating or Waning Gibbous Moon – from October 30th – November 4th passing through Taurus, Gemini, Cancer and into Leo.

This Moon phase sets off with a reasonably calm pace that invites you to mindfully integrate and consolidate your learning from Eclipse season.

The essence of achievement through mindfulness and balance continues into November… in fact, the more balanced you are, i.e. life/work balance… self-care/care of others… heart/mind… logic/emotionality & empathy… the more productive this period will be for you.

The Last Quarter Moon - November 5th – Leo.

The energy today is fast paced and potentially quite deep and emotional.

For everything that's going really well this will feel amazing… but if anything isn't running smoothly don't be carried away in the emotionality of things.

Whatever is taking place in the uniqueness of your world, try to slow it down a bit, get present, and make sure that your thought, words, and actions are all in alignment with everything that you wish to see and manifest in the world.

The Balsamic Moon or Waning Crescent Moon – from November 6th – 12th passing through Virgo, Libra, and into Scorpio.

This Moon phase feels like it may strongly connect you with your desires and the things that really matter to you.

Overall, the Lunar influence can be divided into two halves, the first from the 6th to the 9th where desires are aided by synchronicities and potentially unexpected but useful events and circumstances, and the second between the 10th and the 12th when things hot up a bit with unfulfilled desires calling for expression.

The diminishing Lunar influence offers to soften these dynamics making this a great time for internal observation and journalling.

The New Moon – November 13th - 20° 43' Scorpio.

The planetary collaborations of this Scorpio New Moon are very dynamic, highly emotional, extremely passionate, a bit impulsive… and possibly rather impatient as well.

Given that a Scorpio New Moon naturally lends its energy to support wishes that focus on empowerment through self-mastery, transformation, letting go of power struggles, partnerships, deep Soulmate connections and our sensuality and sexuality… lean into the highest possible perspectives… harness the passion… and place it into dedicated focused wishes with an intention to follow through with actions that commit you fully to your desires.

New Moon Global Timings:

Los Angeles, USA	Mon, 13 Nov 2023 at 01:27 PST
New York, USA	Mon, 13 Nov 2023 at 04:27 EST
Reykjavik, Iceland	Mon, 13 Nov 2023 at 09:27 GMT
London, United Kingdom	Mon, 13 Nov 2023 at 09:27 GMT
Paris, France	Mon, 13 Nov 2023 at 10:27 CET
Cape Town, South Africa	Mon, 13 Nov 2023 at 11:27 SAST
Delhi, India	Mon, 13 Nov 2023 at 14:57 IST
Perth, Australia	Mon, 13 Nov 2023 at 17:27 AWST
Tokyo, Japan	Mon, 13 Nov 2023 at 18:27 JST
Sydney, Australia	Mon, 13 Nov 2023 at 20:27 AEDT
Auckland, New Zealand	Mon, 13 Nov 2023 at 22:27 NZDT
Greenwich Mean Time, GMT	Mon, 13 Nov 2023 at 09:27 GMT

The Waxing Crescent Moon – from November 14th – 19th passing through Sagittarius, Capricorn, and into Aquarius.

Although this Moon phase begins with considerable emotional sensitivity, the Lunar energy soon eases into a steady flow that offers to steer you gently forwards… on the 17th we see a shift in gears with a slightly faster pace picking up but still reasonable steady and supportive of sensible measured expansion.

Given the intensity of the Scorpio New Moon this Moon phase feels refreshingly gentle.

The First Quarter Moon – November 20th - Aquarius.

The Lunar connections today feel like they are just itching to manifest and move ahead, lots of go go go energy with forward motion... but every First Quarter Moon invites a point of review and evaluation, so even if everything in your world is running amazingly well and pushing ahead, take time anyway to just press the pause button, stand back, and take a quick recce... you might be surprised at the benefit of this.

And if anything isn't going as smoothly as you would like, don't be swept along by the underlying feel of the day, slow down, pause, and meditate.

The Waxing Gibbous Moon – from November 21st – 26th passing through Pisces, Aries, and Taurus.

I feel like this Moon phase moves through three distinct mini chapters which when understood and combined can bring some seriously empowering potential to your progress of manifestation.

The first phase has a slightly serious edge to it with emotionality... but also imagination. This could feel creatively empowering with a ton of ideas flowing through, but could also lead to your imagination running wild, so keep this aspect in check and remain grounded.

This leads to a middle phase where signs, signals, and synchronicities will naturally support progress, so be alert to possibility and responsive in the moment.

Finally, the Lunar input supports expansion with the potential to integrate unexpected and out of the box solutions into real solid creative actions.

The Full Moon – November 27th - 4° 51' Gemini.

I feel like this is a Full Moon of testing... and with purpose... a Moon that will ask you questions...

Do you really walk your talk? Do you apply your beliefs to the things that you actually think say and do? Do you hold not only good values but live good values in practice?

A Full Moon almost always signifies a time of heightened emotions. There is a higher vibration and a lower vibration to every emotion that you have... yes even the challenging ones!

Take envy for example... the higher vibrational and empowered response to envy are inspiration and aspiration. You can aspire to be like the person you envy and admire and take action accordingly... yea! However, the lower vibrational and more re-active response to envy brings an acting out of underhanded backstabbing behaviors which are designed to sabotage the reputation and success of the person who is envied... ultimately this will inevitably backfire, shutting down opportunities for the saboteur and reinforcing low self-esteem.

Personally, I plan to set aside time today to listen, to meditate, and with honesty, have a bit of a meeting with myself, and evaluate from the inside out.

Full Moon Global Timings:

Los Angeles, USA	Mon, 27 Nov 2023 at 01:16 PST
New York, USA	Mon, 27 Nov 2023 at 04:16 EST
Reykjavik, Iceland	Mon, 27 Nov 2023 at 09:16 GMT
London, United Kingdom	Mon, 27 Nov 2023 at 09:16 GMT
Paris, France	Mon, 27 Nov 2023 at 10:16 CET
Cape Town, South Africa	Mon, 27 Nov 2023 at 11:16 SAST
Delhi, India	Mon, 27 Nov 2023 at 14:46 IST
Perth, Australia	Mon, 27 Nov 2023 at 17:16 AWST
Tokyo, Japan	Mon, 27 Nov 2023 at 18:16 JST
Sydney, Australia	Mon, 27 Nov 2023 at 20:16 AEDT
Auckland, New Zealand	Mon, 27 Nov 2023 at 22:16 NZDT
Greenwich Mean Time, GMT	Mon, 27 Nov 2023 at 09:16 GMT

The Disseminating or Waning Gibbous Moon – from November 28th into December passing through Gemini and Cancer.

Following such an incredibly powerful Full Moon, in the first few days of this phase the Lunar influence urges and actively supports creative and imaginative solutions that bring about a longer-term vision of balance and harmony.

30 Monday
Taurus / VOC / Gemini

Waning Gibbous Moon Phase Begins

31 Tuesday
Gemini

Festival of Samhain Northern Hemisphere – Beltane Southern Hemisphere

1 Wednesday
Gemini / VOC / Cancer

2 Thursday
Cancer

3 Friday
Cancer

Journaling and Notes

4 Saturday
Cancer / VOC / Leo

Waning Gibbous Moon Phase Ends
Saturn Retrograde Ends

5 Sunday
Leo

Last Quarter Moon Leo

6 Monday
Leo / VOC / Virgo

Waning Crescent Moon Phase Begins

7 Tuesday
Virgo

8 Wednesday
Virgo

9 Thursday
Virgo / VOC / Libra

10 Friday
Libra

Veterans Day – Public Holiday USA

Journaling and Notes

11 Saturday

Libra / VOC / Scorpio

Veterans Day USA

12 Sunday

Scorpio

Waning Crescent Moon Phase Ends

13 Monday
Scorpio / VOC

New Moon 20°43' Scorpio

14 Tuesday
VOC / Sagittarius

Waxing Crescent Moon Phase Begins

15 Wednesday
Sagittarius / VOC

16 Thursday
VOC / Capricorn

17 Friday
Capricorn

Journaling and Notes

18 **Saturday**

Capricorn / VOC / Aquarius

19 **Sunday**

Aquarius

Waxing Crescent Moon Phase Ends

20 Monday
Aquarius / VOC / Pisces

First Quarter Moon Aquarius

21 Tuesday
Pisces

Waxing Gibbous Moon Phase Begins

22 Wednesday
Pisces / VOC / Aries

Sun Enters Sagittarius

23 Thursday
Aries

Thanksgiving Day - USA

24 Friday
Aries / VOC / Taurus

Journaling and Notes

25 Saturday

Taurus

26 Sunday

Taurus / VOC

Waxing Gibbous Moon Phase Ends

27 Monday
VOC / Gemini

Full Moon 4°51’ Gemini

28 Tuesday
Gemini

Waning Gibbous Moon Phase Begins

29 Wednesday
Gemini / VOC / Cancer

30 Thursday
Cancer

1 Friday
Cancer / VOC / Leo

Journaling and Notes

2 Saturday

Leo

3 Sunday

Leo

Desires, Goals, and Intentions for December 2023

Welcome to December 2023

December 2023. Embrace the joy of living!

This month feels like a breath of fresh air with a definite emphasis on positivity, growth, and creative, imaginative potential. Almost as if you get to reset your energetic compass, wrap a few things up... (excuse the Christmas pun) bring some things to completion, and still drive some more stuff forwards, whilst going with the flow.

Although three of the bigger players all move into a forward motion during this month, Neptune on the 6th, Chiron on the 27th, and Jupiter on the 31st, Mercury begins a period of retrograde on the 14th through to 2nd January, which often tends to bring interruptions and slow things down. Uranus also remains on a retrograde pathway until 27th January bringing innovation and opportunity, so an interesting mix.

The New Moon in Sagittarius on the 12th and 13th is super super nice in every possible way and the Full Moon in Cancer on the 26th and 27th is absolutely primed to support you in fixing problems through listening to your intuition and using your creative imagination.

So with the turning point of the Winter Solstice in the northern hemisphere and the Summer Solstice in the southern hemisphere lean into this pivotal point of shift and re-balance, re-energize, re-align, and celebrate an extraordinary year of Soul growth.

And then get set for a whole New Year of potential and possibility!

Our cards of Be Your Brilliant Self and Walk your Talk invite you to get present and be the best that you can be, and both Thurisaz the Rune of Gateway, and Berkana the Rune of growth, honor an appropriate pause before starting the New Year afresh.

The card of Be Your Brilliant Self reminds you how extraordinary life truly is and urges you to get present and connect with humility to all that you have right now. Combined with Thurisaz the Rune of Gateway, you are invited to pause and review, casting your mind back over all your experiences of the year, the good and the more challenging, and then with gratitude for all of the learning, prepare to step into the new.

Additional messages and guidance.
This card invites you to become present to the magnificence of the everyday things and the endless opportunities that you have, to be extraordinary, in an ordinary way.

Each day we say and do a multitude of things, many of which take place on autopilot. Whether you are involved in a simple task such as hanging the washing on the line, or you are engaged in something that is seemingly bigger, such as holding an important meeting or conversation, you are asked to place equal importance in all of your actions and activities, engaging in everything to the very best of your ability.

Cards and Runes December 2023

The card of Walk your Talk aligning with Berkana the Rune of growth and re-birth invites you to make a commitment to stepping up and becoming the very best version of you, thinking, being, and doing, all that you wish to see in the world, in the coming year.

Additional messages and guidance.
Congruence and authenticity are words that are commonly used and yet walking our talk and truly aligning all aspects of our lives with our core inner value can be easier said than done, particularly in the face of situations/people/environments that hold an entirely different perspective or operate on an entirely different basis.

This card asks you align yourself, with yourself. Not the construction of the ego self, who feels compelled to comply to the constraints and perspectives of those around you, whether they resonate with you or not, but to align yourself with your deepest inner voice, the voice of your soul.

Moon Phases December 2023

The Disseminating or Waning Gibbous Moon – from November 28th - December 4th passing through Gemini, Cancer, Leo and into Virgo.

Following such an incredibly powerful Full Moon, in the first few days of this phase the Lunar influence urges and actively supports creative and imaginative solutions that bring about a longer-term vision of balance and harmony.

As we move into December we see a spike of Lunar intensity on the 1st so if things aren't moving as fast as you would like, be sure to keep your emotions in check, this is fleeting. The overall Lunar flow of this phase is fairly steady.

Be open to potential spontaneity on the 3rd and as the Moon moves into Virgo the influence of the Moon supports a more serious outlook when diligence and attention to detail will pay off.

The Last Quarter Moon - December 5th – Virgo.

Aided by our beautiful First Quarter Moon in Virgo, the overall astro-dynamics of the day suggest a push of energy that is arriving to highlight what you need to do to move you in the right direction.

This could be loaded with motivation and forward movement, but if this isn't feeling particularly expansive for you, it may be that the direction indicated is to slow down, get still and notice the smaller stuff. Sometimes choosing not to do something is actually the most active response that's needed.

The Balsamic Moon or Waning Crescent Moon – from December 6th – 11th passing through Virgo, Libra, Scorpio, and into Sagittarius.

As the Lunar energy gently slows down and diminishes, fall into flow with this dynamic. This feels like a Moon phase when even if you feel pressure to drive forwards, slowing down may actually generate far greater productivity.

With potential openings happening on the 9th and 10th, a gentle pace will help you to be more present to these opportunities. So go with the flow, enjoy the overall energetic of gentleness, and wherever possible, let the tide steer you.

The New Moon – December 12th / 13th - 20° 39' Sagittarius.

The flow of energy on this New Moon today is SUPER SUPER NICE... in every way!

A New Moon in Sagittarius naturally invites you to surround your wishes and intentions with positivity, determination, and grace, and the overall astro-dynamics today bring a collaboration of energy that is primed to expand your desires and lift you into high vibrational thoughts and feelings, bringing hope, optimism, and the finding of solutions.

These energetics also naturally enhance any wishes that connect with your personal sense of freedom, the rights and freedom of others, truth, liberty, and justice.

Wishes set at this time are also perfect in bringing increased motivation, with stamina to see something through. Yea!

New Moon Global Timings:

Los Angeles, USA	Tue, 12 Dec 2023 at 15:31 PST
New York, USA	Tue, 12 Dec 2023 at 18:31 EST
Reykjavik, Iceland	Tue, 12 Dec 2023 at 23:31 GMT
London, United Kingdom	Tue, 12 Dec 2023 at 23:31 GMT
Paris, France	Wed, 13 Dec 2023 at 00:31 CET
Cape Town, South Africa	Wed, 13 Dec 2023 at 01:31 SAST
Delhi, India	Wed, 13 Dec 2023 at 05:01 IST
Perth, Australia	Wed, 13 Dec 2023 at 07:31 AWST
Tokyo, Japan	Wed, 13 Dec 2023 at 08:31 JST
Sydney, Australia	Wed, 13 Dec 2023 at 10:31 AEDT
Auckland, New Zealand	Wed, 13 Dec 2023 at 12:31 NZDT
Greenwich Mean Time, GMT	Tue, 12 Dec 2023 at 23:31 GMT

The Waxing Crescent Moon – from December 14th – 18th passing through Capricorn, Aquarius, and into Pisces.

This positivity of the New Moon predominantly continues throughout this phase bringing a flow of excitement and a buzz of anticipation... so truly jump on board with this and make the most of the harmonious planetary collaborations at this time. And by all means, relax and enjoy, but also, as the Lunar energy builds, choose to invest in productivity as well.

The First Quarter Moon – December 19th - Pisces.

A First Quarter Moon naturally invites review, and the overall astro-dynamics of the day are bringing the perfect conditions for evaluation, adjustments, and transformations.

If you find that your circumstances are causing you to have to consider some big changes and you are a bit wobbly about quite how best to approach this, then simply notice and validate what needs to change and then open yourself to receive further support as to how to proceed.

The Waxing Gibbous Moon – from December 20th – 25th passing through Aries, Taurus, Gemini, and into Cancer.

The overall flow of this Moon phase feels very 'onwards and upwards' which in your manifestations is going to feel great if you yourself are feeling on top of the world and in a get go place.

Interestingly, even if you are needing to move at a more gentle and steady pace, the overall Lunar influence seems sufficiently steady enough to support you to stay on track regardless, with pockets of stability surrounding any brief surges of heightened emotionality.

And as always, emotions will rise just before the Full Moon, so be alert to what you are shown at this time.

The Full Moon – December 26th / 27th - 4° 57' Cancer.

The overall astro-dynamics today are absolutely primed to support you in fixing problems through listening to your intuition and using your creative imagination.

A Full Moon in Cancer will naturally invite you to become an observer of your life and to notice what you need to change and release to nurture a solid strong internal foundation of self-esteem built on true self-value and self-respect, illuminating pathways of healing and regeneration making space for the new to emerge.

Use your Full Moon illuminations and insights to see exactly what you need to do to build a bridge of steady growth, nurture, and kindness, to carry you forwards into a New Year of opportunity and possibilities.

Full Moon Global Timings:

Los Angeles, USA	Tue, 26 Dec 2023 at 16:32 PST
New York, USA	Tue, 26 Dec 2023 at 19:32 EST
Reykjavik, Iceland	Wed, 27 Dec 2023 at 00:32 GMT
London, United Kingdom	Wed, 27 Dec 2023 at 00:32 GMT
Paris, France	Wed, 27 Dec 2023 at 01:32 CET
Cape Town, South Africa	Wed, 27 Dec 2023 at 02:32 SAST
Delhi, India	Wed, 27 Dec 2023 at 06:02 IST
Perth, Australia	Wed, 27 Dec 2023 at 08:32 AWST
Tokyo, Japan	Wed, 27 Dec 2023 at 09:32 JST
Sydney, Australia	Wed, 27 Dec 2023 at 11:32 AEDT
Auckland, New Zealand	Wed, 27 Dec 2023 at 13:32 NZDT
Greenwich Mean Time, GMT	Wed, 27 Dec 2023 at 00:32 GMT

The Disseminating or Waning Gibbous Moon – from December 28th into January 2024 passing through Cancer, Leo, and Virgo.

Creativity rules the day in the first part of this Moon phase.

Given that the overall dynamics of 2023 have been extraordinary in their potential to rocket your consciousness, as we approach a New Year, take time to celebrate where you are right now, and adopting an attitude of inner critique rather than inner criticism, (there is a massive difference) validate all you have achieved and dream into a picture of everything you wish to create and manifest in the coming year of 2024.

December 2023

4 Monday
Leo / VOC / Virgo

Waning Gibbous Moon Phase Ends

5 Tuesday
Virgo

Last Quarter Moon Virgo

6 Wednesday
Virgo / VOC / Libra

Waning Crescent Moon Phase Begins
Neptune Retrograde Ends

7 Thursday
Libra

8 Friday
Libra

Journaling and Notes

9 Saturday

Libra / VOC / Scorpio

10 Sunday

Scorpio

11 Monday
Scorpio / VOC / Sagittarius

Waning Crescent Moon Phase Ends

12 Tuesday
Sagittarius

New Moon 20°39’ Sagittarius

13 Wednesday
Sagittarius / VOC / Capricorn

New Moon 20°39’ Sagittarius
Mercury Retrograde Begins

14 Thursday
Capricorn

Waxing Crescent Moon Phase Begins

15 Friday
Capricorn / VOC / Aquarius

Journaling and Notes

16 Saturday

Aquarius

17 Sunday

Aquarius / VOC / Pisces

18 Monday

Pisces

Waxing Crescent Moon Phase Ends

19 Tuesday

Pisces / VOC / Aquarius

First Quarter Moon Pisces

20 Wednesday

Aries

Waxing Gibbous Moon Phase Begins

21 Thursday

Aries

22 Friday

Aries / VOC / Taurus

Sun Enters Capricorn
Winter Solstice Northern Hemisphere – Summer Solstice Southern Hemisphere

Journaling and Notes

23 Saturday

Taurus

24 Sunday

Taurus / VOC / Gemini

Christmas Eve

25 Monday
Gemini

Waxing Gibbous Moon Phase Ends
Christmas Day

26 Tuesday
Gemini / VOC / Cancer

St Stephens Day Ireland
Full Moon 4°57' Cancer
Boxing Day

27 Wednesday
Cancer

Full Moon 4°57' Cancer
Chiron Retrograde Ends

28 Thursday
Cancer / VOC

Waning Gibbous Moon Phase Begins

29 Friday
VOC / Leo

Journaling and Notes

30 Saturday
Leo

31 Sunday
Leo / VOC / Virgo

Jupiter Retrograde Ends
New Year's Eve

1 Monday

Virgo

2 Tuesday

Virgo / VOC

Waning Gibbous Moon Phase Ends
Mercury Retrograde Ends

3 Wednesday

VOC / Libra

Last Quarter Moon Libra

4 Thursday

Libra

Last Quarter Moon Libra

5 Friday

Libra / VOC / Scorpio

Waning Crescent Moon Phase Begins

Journaling and Notes

6 Saturday

Scorpio

7 Sunday

Scorpio / VOC / Sagittarius

New Year Wishes and Intentions for 2024

Happy Manifesting in 2024!

The Moon in the Zodiac Signs

Moon in Aries.

At this emotionally powerful time, use the energy to be assertive and to initiate your ideas. Say how it is and take action.

Moon in Taurus.

Grounded, sensual, and earthy, use this energy to attune yourself with the natural rhythms of nature. A great time for walking meditations.

Moon in Gemini.

A time of communication, reaching out and connecting with others, use this energy for networking and socializing.

Moon in Cancer.

A wonderful time to be at home, share food and be in the company of family and close friends. Use this energy to nourish your soul, spending time with those you love.

Moon in Leo.

Sing, laugh, express yourself and find your voice. Use this energy to feel alive and embrace the joy of self-discovery and self-expression. We are never too old to play!

Moon in Virgo.

This energy supports us in attending to any work that requires dedication, structure, order and precision. Approach your tasks with willingness and a desire to serve.

Moon in Libra.

The energy of this Moon calls us to seek harmony and to find balance. This is a time to share and to discover ourselves through our relationships and the company of others.

Moon in Scorpio.

A time to journey inwards, this energy connects us to the depths of our unconscious and can bring deep emotions to the surface. Be sure to listen to yourself and take your yearnings seriously.

Moon in Sagittarius.

The energy of this Moon invites us to vision in an optimistic future, full of hope and possibility. A great time to expand our horizons and dream big!

Moon in Capricorn.

The energy of this Moon invites us to take pragmatic, practical actions to manifest our ideas into form. Get building and embrace the joy of doing.

Moon in Aquarius.

A time to collaborate, share ideas and work together. The energy of this Moon invites you to align your individual contribution with a higher vision of greater purpose that will also serve the collective Soul of humanity.

Moon in Pisces.

A time to dream and a time to heal. Open yourself to divine inspiration and allow yourself to be guided. The energy of this Moon brings illumination, fuelling imagination and creativity.

VOC - Void of Course Moon

As the Moon travels around our planet from our viewpoint here on Earth, she passes through each of the 12 signs of the zodiac. When the Moon is 'Void of Course', (VOC) it means that she is transitioning through the space in between two different signs. This can last for minutes, or sometimes several hours.

As she travels through each of the Zodiac signs her energy is channeled through the energetic resonance or personality of that sign. However, when she is Void of Course, there is a kind of energetic pause where her energy is no longer affected or guided by the influence of a particular sign.

I have noticed that this space of 'in betweenness' affects people in quite different and uniquely individual ways, depending on how they are feeling and what is taking place in the immediacy of their lives at any given time.

For some, this space in between can feel quite liberating, creating a natural channel for insights, illuminations, and even increased motivation to flow through. However, for others, particularly during periods of extreme change and transition, the void of course Moon can feel a bit unanchored and directionless.

I have personally found it really helpful to notice how the void of course space affects me and incredibly empowering to be aware ahead of time of any particularly long void of course periods.

For up-to-date Void of Course Moon information follow Jenny on social media

- https://www.youtube.com/c/MoonMagicWeeklyTarot
- https://www.facebook.com/MoonMagicJennyFlorence
- https://www.instagram.com/moonmagicjennyflorence/

Solar and Lunar Eclipses

During eclipse season, the already intense energy of both the New and Full Moons are intensified. An eclipse in your sign, will always be a significant trigger point or turning point in your own personal process of evolution and can often herald random events that create sudden and unexpected changes.

On your personal journey of manifestation, understanding this heightened and intensified energy is incredibly helpful in knowing when to reflect and set your intentions, and when to take action to move something forwards, particularly if you intend to make or initiate significant changes in any aspect of your life.

Eclipses are also associated with our Karmic journey, creating an energetic rift that overrides our usual perception of and connection to time. The energy of the eclipses is said to open an energetic portal that connects past, present, and future, highlighting your purpose and calling in this present lifetime.

Symbolized in the tarot pack by the cards of Death and the Tower, the energy of both the solar and lunar eclipses are associated with transformation, either internally or in the circumstances of our external lives, and often involves both endings and new beginnings.

I think the best way to work with the influence of the eclipses, is rather than trying to control events, consciously make time to slow down, get still, and practice the art of allowing... let the Universe show you the way, whilst being responsive and taking action as needed.

Solar Eclipse.

A solar eclipse is when the Moon sits in between the Sun and the Earth, with the Moon covering the Sun. This will always occur at a New Moon. The energy associated with this time is the same as a New Moon, but intensified, like a New Moon on steroids!

This is the perfect time to get still and to meditate into a space of personal dreamtime and allow your ideas to flow.

The energy of the solar eclipse can bring an extraordinary surge of creative possibilities, although these may not always arrive in the shape or form that you expect, so if you're already involved in setting wishes and intentions, but then find that something happens to suddenly create a shift in your direction, trust that this unexpected change is important to your personal growth and evolution and connected to the calling of your soul. In matters of manifestation, the universe will always have the upper hand and tends to bring us what we need... although not always what we want!

When you can trust that even in moments of upheaval and disruption you are being gifted with an opportunity, you open yourself to receive the fullest potential and the greatest learning to be found in every situation.

Lunar Eclipse.

A lunar eclipse is when the earth sits between the Moon and the Sun, and this will always occur at a Full Moon. Full Moons are associated with heightened emotions and during a lunar eclipse, emotions can run high, like a Full Moon on steroids!

If we think of the Moon as our Feminine Guardian who circles our planet, gathering the energy of the Sun and redistributing it to the Earth in various measures, at the time of a Lunar Eclipse, the energy of the Moon is like a fully charged battery, highly charged and ready to ignite change.

In the illumination of the Full Moon at her most powerful, all is revealed.

Anything and everything that is running smoothly and working in service of a balanced and authentic life will be apparent to you, confirming that you are walking the right path. Likewise, anything and everything that is not working for you or no longer serving you, both internally and externally, will also be brought into the light, calling to be addressed, changed, and if necessary, released.

As long as something remains hidden or unconscious, you are helpless to address the issue and to take actions of resolution, but when you identify a problem, the very fact that you can see the issue clearly creates an opportunity to seek solutions and find ways forward.

On your personal journey of manifestation, the energy of a lunar eclipse increases your connections with any emotional residue from the past that may be clinging and coloring your perspectives inappropriately, creating an amazing opportunity for cleansing and release, clearing the way for resolution and healing. This is a powerful time to embrace forgiveness, of both yourself and others.

If you are struggling with any difficult emotions this book will help you to understand your Emotions as a source of empowerment… yes… even the tough ones!

- Mindfulness meets Emotional Awareness - 7 Steps to Learn the Language of your Emotions - https://www.amazon.com/author/jennyflorence

Lunar eclipses are also often associated with external changes that are a mirror or a reflection of our internal growth and learning, so whatever is taking place around you, if something in your life appears to be needing to change or to leave, let go gracefully and know that it is timely to the evolution of your soul.

If you are naturally a highly empathic person and particularly sensitive to the feelings of others, at the time of a lunar eclipse you may find yourself highly absorbent to the emotional states of the people around you. Be sure to cleanse and do a daily release ceremony to let go of anything that doesn't belong to you before meditating into your own space of illumination.

- **20th April – 04.12 GMT - New Moon Solar Eclipse 29°49' Aries**
- **5th May – 17.33 GMT - Full Moon Lunar Eclipse 14°57' Scorpio**
- **14th October – 17.54 GMT - New Moon Solar Eclipse 21°07' Libra**
- **28th October – 20.23 GMT Full Moon Lunar Eclipse 5°08' Taurus**

The Planets in Retrograde 2023

The Inner Planets, Mercury, Venus, and Mars.

Mercury in Retrograde.

- **29th December 2022 24° Capricorn – 18th January 2023 08° Capricorn**
- **21st April 15° Taurus – 15th May 05° Taurus**
- **23rd August 21° Virgo – 15th September 08° Virgo**
- **13th December 08° Capricorn – 2nd January 2024 22° Sagittarius**

The energy of Mercury in retrograde is often associated with obstructions and delays, and in a target and goal orientated culture, it is often viewed through a very negative lens. Mercury retrograde periods seem to cause us no end of disruption, plans go astray, we experience roadblocks and diversions, and there are often difficulties with IT and communication systems… however, if you step away from this viewpoint and consider that all aspects of planetary influences are bringing valuable and necessary gifts, this shift in perspective means you can stand back and work with the incoming energy.

If there's a block or diversion, the universe may be giving you an important sign, perhaps you are meant to take an alternative route where you will discover something that was absolutely essential to your personal growth and evolution.

If something from your past raises its head during a Mercury retrograde period, then your attention is required. This is an invitation for you to acknowledge this issue and take the time to do whatever is needed to lay it to rest.

The influence of Mercury invites you to develop wisdom at a level of Soul growth and evolution, so when this planet appears to travel backwards, the energy is calling you to slow down, take your time, and be alert to any signals and signs that the universe is trying to bring you.

This is not the time to plough forwards and to push and to strive… this will come soon enough and if you use the retrograde period well you will be wiser and better placed to move ahead with ease.

Venus in Retrograde.

- **23rd July 28° Leo – 4th September 12° Leo**

Are you in balance? Do you allow yourself to receive as much as you give and vice versa? Are you actively involved in your own self-care? Do you pause to celebrate your achievements along the way, and do you give yourself an appropriate amount of time out to relax?

Self-care is not an act of selfishness; it is an act of consciousness. When Venus moves into retrograde the energy of the feminine invites you to listen to your heart, to override the demands of a busy mind and be centered in your truest values, including and especially your own self-care.

Venus is in retrograde is a wonderful time to reflect and to realign and rebalance all areas of your life. This revitalizing influence will keep your energy clean and flowing and ensure that your energetic resonance is congruent with all that you wish to manifest into the world. As such, Venus in retrograde plays an essential role in your ability to manifest your truest desires.

During periods of transition, if you have ever found yourself questioning what your true calling might be, when Venus is in retrograde, ask for guidance and be open to receive.

If during this time you find yourself called to stand up for your values, the female warrior energy of Venus will support you in connecting with the lioness within. In the name of kindness, compassion and peace, her retrograde energy will encourage you to find your authentic voice, speak your truth, and stand firm in your boundaries.

Mars in Retrograde.

- **30th October 2022 25° Gemini – 12th January 08° Gemini**

When Mars moves into a retrograde motion you are invites to reassess your progress, not only the projects, relationships, and circumstances of your external world, but also the way that you set about acquiring and achieving these goals.

Mars in retrograde will often highlight the role that certain emotions play in the process of manifestation, for example, anger when channeled positively through mindful considered actions creates assertiveness, however, its negative counterpart can result in aggression and frustration being directed inappropriately, towards both ourselves and others. So, during this time, be prepared to journey inwards and reassess your needs and desires but also how you get these met… working from the inside out.

The Transpersonal Planets, Jupiter, and Saturn.

Jupiter in Retrograde.

- **4th September 15° Taurus – 31st December 05° Taurus**

This is a time of powerful personal growth! Jupiter in retrograde invites you on an inward quest of self-discovery seeking the knowledge and illumination so you can stand in your own truth and walk your talk.

Jupiter is known as the planet of good luck and good fortune and from the perspective of manifestation, during the retrograde period can bring experiences that invite you to look within and seek answers of a Spiritual nature, helping you to forge your true values and attune with your greater purpose. And so, during this period windows of opportunity may open that illuminate issues from your past, including past lives, giving you the opportunity to find resolution and align with your true calling at this present moment of your journey. Any internal growth and changes made during this time will then in turn, manifest outwardly when Jupiter returns to a forward flow of expansion. Seriously amazing stuff!

Saturn in Retrograde.

- **17th June 07° Pisces – 4th November 0°30' Pisces**

Saturn is known as Father Time and the planet of Karma and when his energy moves into retrograde, aspects of your life that need restructuring and reorganizing will come to a head and circumstances will show you exactly what is working for you... as well as anything that is not!

For us as humans, the lessons of Saturn can feel quite harsh as the energy calls us to account, speaking in the name of "Tough Love", however, this is not without major rewards! The more open you are to embracing the natural evolutionary process of "weeding and pruning", letting go gracefully of anything that no longer serves or has outlived its purpose, whether these are physical aspects of your life or internal attitudes and beliefs, then the more smoothly these periods of profound transition will emerge.

Saturn retrograde energy is a reminder that change is both necessary and natural and that we live in a continual space of learning, not only from all the amazing experiences that fill us with joy, but also from the experiences that don't feel so good as well!

From the perspective of manifestation, when you recognize that all your experiences, both good and bad, are a source of inspiration and guidance, then rather than dwell on the negative, you can use every experience to define your desires with greater clarity. This in turn opens us to receive the guidance and direction that we need to manifest those desires that resonate with us at a core level of Soul.

The Outer Planets, Uranus, Neptune, and Pluto.

The energy of the outer planets is slow moving which means that their influence is deep and penetrating creating significant growth stages with long term implications. In our individual natal charts, the positioning of these planets will not only have personal implications but will also be an indicator of generational traits.

Uranus in Retrograde.

- **24th August 2022 18° Taurus – 22nd January 14° Taurus**
- **29th August 23° Taurus – 27th January 2024 19° Taurus**

Uranus is known as the Great Awakener and the bringer of sudden events that wake you up and let you know that something needs to change. Uranus energy also holds a direction of higher purpose with out of the box solutions.

When in retrograde, this sometimes-impulsive energy slows down and invites you to take conscious innovative actions that forge new ways of being and living, all with the purpose of liberating you from limiting perspectives and aligning your manifestations the greater good.

Neptune in Retrograde.

- **30th June 27° Pisces – 6th December 24° Pisces**

Neptune is the planet of creativity, dreams, and imagination and as such plays a key role in manifestation.

Being so dreamy, the influence of Neptunian energy opens you to divine guidance and spiritual illumination, however… it can also bring so much dreamy energy that you may find it hard to remain grounded or hold your boundaries. This is valuable to know as Neptunian energy can sometimes create vulnerability around people who operate through delusion and deception.

When in retrograde, the Neptunian energy calls us to get real… and this is FAB!

Neptune in retrograde brings heightened levels of intuition and illumination… it's like a kind of Spiritual Reality check that helps you to see beyond any false illusions that may have previously been holding you back.

These powerful insights can be used to bring clarity of purpose and intent, releasing limiting beliefs and perspectives that may have previously blocked some of your manifestations.

Pluto in Retrograde.

- **1st May 0°21' Aquarius – 11th October 27° Capricorn**

Pluto requests transformation and re-birth and naturally invites personal reflection at its most powerful. This influence will tap into your psychological make-up through a deep dive into your unconscious, revealing any shadows from the past that need to be released, purifying, and emerging afresh with greater vitality and potency.

When Pluto is in retrograde it is not a time to hold onto or cling to the past. If some aspect of your world seems to be coming to an end, whether internal or external, such as any outdated thinking patterns or behaviors, an inappropriate or limiting belief, or an actual situation or person, let go gracefully and allow yourself to emerge into a space of new beginnings.

Chiron and the Consciousness of Healing.

Chiron in Retrograde.

- **23rd July 19° Aries – 27th December 15° Aries**

Chiron embodies the classic architype of the wounded healer. In mythology he is depicted as half man and half beast, able to bring wisdom and to teach and heal others and yet he cannot heal himself. As an outer influence, his energy is slow moving, signifying profound generational changes.

Astrologically, Chiron is not a planet, but a comet, whose presence here is transient. In spiritual circles it is said that his presence will create a rainbow bridge to lead humanity to a higher plane of consciousness, so we can stand in equality, not just with one another, but in unity with all of life. Many Tribal cultures hold legends that speak of all of the life on this planet arriving on the tail of a comet, acknowledging that from a spiritual perspective we all come from the same source and are all equal.

The retrograde energy of Chiron invites you to into a space of deep cleansing and repair, laying the past to rest and stepping into a space of unity and higher vision.

This level of healing has the potential for individuals and all of us as a collective humanity to resolve long standing historical wounds that have spanned generations, bringing a new and different future for our planet and generations yet to come.

The Art of Manifestation Oracle Cards

The Art of Manifestation Oracle Cards featured in this diary are available to buy on Amazon.

About the Author

Jenny Florence is a best-selling Author. Her career as a professional Accredited BACP, UKRC Registered Counsellor spanned over 28 years working with individuals, couples, and teams.

She is the founder and creator of the A-Z of Emotional Health on-line Video Library, a free Public Resource, dedicated to understanding Emotional and Mental Wellness from a holistic perspective.

She has been reading Tarot cards and Runes since she was a teenager and has also studied astrology.

For more information visit her Free on-line Library;
https://www.azemotionalhealth.com/

Her books and cards include:

- 7 Steps to Spiritual Empathy – Learn to Listen, Change your Life!
- Mindfulness meets Emotional Awareness - 7 Steps to Learn the Language of your Emotions
- I Choose Love – the A-Z Guidebook for the Spiritual Warrior
- Manifest with the Moon Astro-Moon Diary and Journal
- The Art of Manifestation Oracle Cards.

You can order her books and cards via your local bookstore or from Amazon.

To watch free monthly tutorials and support Jenny's ongoing work join Patreon

- https://www.patreon.com/AZEmotionalHealth

To access Lunar updates, Webinars, and Readings follow Jenny on social media.

- https://www.youtube.com/c/MoonMagicWeeklyTarot
- https://www.facebook.com/MoonMagicJennyFlorence
- https://www.instagram.com/moonmagicjennyflorence/

Printed in Great Britain
by Amazon

16298167R00131